Developing Your Teaching

Packed with advice, vignettes and case studies, as well as useful tips and checklists for improving teaching, the second edition of *Developing Your Teaching* is the ideal toolkit to support the development of teaching practice. Providing a blend of ideas, interactive review points and case study examples from university teachers, this accessible handbook for professional practice provides ideas on a range of topics including:

- learning from student feedback and peer review
- students as consumers and their expectations
- building effective partnerships with students and colleagues
- developing a teaching portfolio
- choosing effective teaching practices
- the challenges and benefits of securing an initial teacher qualification

A must-read for all those new to teaching in higher education, as well as more experienced lecturers looking to refresh and advance the quality of their teaching, this fully updated new edition is the ideal toolkit to support the development of teaching practice.

Peter Kahn is the Director of the Centre for Higher Education Studies at the University of Liverpool, UK.

Lorraine Anderson is an Assistant Director of Student Services and Head of the Academic Skills Centre at the University of Dundee, UK.

Key Guides for Effective Teaching in Higher Education Series
Edited by Kate Exley

This indispensable series is aimed at new lecturers, postgraduate students who have teaching time, Graduate Teaching Assistants, part-time tutors and demonstrators, as well as experienced teaching staff who may feel it's time to review their skills in teaching and learning.

Titles in this series will provide the teacher in higher education with practical, realistic guidance on the various different aspects of their teaching role, which is underpinned not only by current research in the field, but also by the extensive experience of individual authors, and with a keen eye kept on the limitations and opportunities therein. By bridging a gap between academic theory and practice, all titles will provide generic guidance on teaching, learning and assessment issues, which is then brought to life through the use of short, illustrative examples drawn from a range of disciplines. All titles in the series will:

- represent up-to-date thinking and incorporate the use of computing and information technology (C&IT) where appropriate
- consider methods and approaches for teaching and learning when there is an increasing diversity in learning and a growth in student numbers
- encourage reflexive practice and self-evaluation, and a means of developing the skills of teaching, learning and assessment
- provide links and references to other work on the topic and research evidence where appropriate.

Titles in the series will prove invaluable whether they are used for self-study or as part of a formal induction programme on teaching in higher education (HE), and will also be of relevance to teaching staff working in further education (FE) settings.

Other titles in this series:

Leading Learning and Teaching in Higher Education: The Key Guide to Designing and Delivering Courses
 – Doug Parkin
Using Technology to Support Learning and Teaching
 – Andy Fisher, Kate Exley, Dragos Ciobanu
Giving a Lecture: From Presenting to Teaching
 – Kate Exley and Reg Dennick
Inclusion and Diversity: Meeting the Needs of all Students
 – Sue Grace and Phil Gravestock

Developing Your Teaching

Towards Excellence

Second Edition

Peter Kahn
and
Lorraine Anderson

LONDON AND NEW YORK

Second edition published 2019
by Routledge
2 Park Square, Milton Park, Abingdon, Oxon, OX14 4RN

and by Routledge
52 Vanderbilt Avenue, New York, NY 10017

Routledge is an imprint of the Taylor & Francis Group, an informa business

© 2019 Peter Kahn and Lorraine Anderson

The right of Peter Kahn and Lorraine Anderson to be identified as authors of this work has been asserted by them in accordance with sections 77 and 78 of the Copyright, Designs and Patents Act 1988.

All rights reserved. No part of this book may be reprinted or reproduced or utilised in any form or by any electronic, mechanical, or other means, now known or hereafter invented, including photocopying and recording, or in any information storage or retrieval system, without permission in writing from the publishers.

Trademark notice: Product or corporate names may be trademarks or registered trademarks, and are used only for identification and explanation without intent to infringe.

First edition published by Routledge 2006

British Library Cataloguing-in-Publication Data
A catalogue record for this book is available from the British Library

Library of Congress Cataloging-in-Publication Data
Names: Kahn, Peter (Peter E.), author.
Title: Developing your teaching : towards excellence / Peter Kahn and Lorraine Anderson.
Other titles: Effective teaching in higher education.
Description: Second edition. | New York : Routledge, 2019. | Series: Key guides for effective teaching in higher education series | "First edition published by Routledge 2006"—T.p. verso. | Includes index.
Identifiers: LCCN 2018050596 | ISBN 9781138591189 (Hardback) | ISBN 9781138591196 (Paperback) | ISBN 9780429490583 (EBook)
Subjects: LCSH: College teaching. | Learning.
Classification: LCC LB2331 .K245 2019 | DDC 378.1/25—dc23
LC record available at https://lccn.loc.gov/2018050596

ISBN: 978–1-138–59118–9 (hbk)
ISBN: 978–1-138–59119–6 (pbk)
ISBN: 978–0-429–49058–3 (ebk)

Typeset in Perpetua
by Apex CoVantage, LLC

Contents

List of figures and tables viii
List of case studies ix
Acknowledgements xi
Series editor introduction xiii

1 Introduction: The teaching landscape 1
   Introduction 1
   The discipline of noticing 5
   Flying the flag 7
   Realising excellence – concept and practice 7
   Conclusions 8

2 Choosing effective teaching practices 10
   Introduction 10
   Evidence from experience 10
   Drawing ideas from others 17
   The written word 20
   Gaining from research 20
   Conclusion: Beyond what is rational 23

3 The discipline as a locus for enhancement 27
   Introduction 27
   Connecting with your subject 27
   Disciplines as spaces for dialogue 34
   Disciplines that evolve 38
   Conclusions 42

4 A partnership with students in learning and teaching 45
   Introduction 45
   Students as co-creators 46
   Students as teachers 57

	Opportunities and challenges	60
	Conclusions	63
5	Engaging with reflective practice	66
	Introduction	66
	Identifying reflective practice	66
	Developing your teaching through reflective practice	70
	Conclusions	81
6	Shifting collective practice	85
	Introduction	85
	Foci for collective practice	86
	The centrality of relationships	89
	Seeing it through	93
	Conclusions	98
7	Connecting to drivers	100
	Introduction	100
	Working with drivers	101
	Identifying drivers for positive change	113
	Conclusions	114
8	Researching your own practice	116
	Introduction: Making a difference	116
	Making a start with evaluation	118
	And then moving into research	121
	Socialising your research	126
	Conclusions	128
9	Taking a lead in teaching	131
	Introduction	131
	Securing a role	132
	Taking on leadership	135
	Conclusions	144
10	Understanding teaching excellence	146
	Introduction	146
	Exploring teaching excellence	147
	A lens on teaching excellence	155
	Deliberate Practice – an accessible route to excellence?	155
	Aspiring to excellence in teaching and learning	158
	Conclusions	163
11	Career-wide enhancement	166
	Introduction	166
	Taking an enhancement-led approach to career-wide learning	167

	Taking advantage of opportunities and going wide	175
	Conclusions	180
12	Conclusion: A sense of direction	185
	Introduction	185
	Developing your teaching: An ongoing story	186
	The road goes ever on and on	191
	Glossary	193
	Index	199

Figures and Tables

FIGURES

1.1	Models of teacher professional development	5
4.1	Student partnership journey in learning and teaching	46
4.2	Ladder of student participation in curriculum design	54
5.1	Aspects of reflective learning	68
6.1	A review of your professional networks	91
7.1	Drivers that impact practice	102
9.1	The Johari Window	133
10.1	How do I know?	150
10.2	Triangulation of perspectives on developing excellence through Teaching and Learning Fellowships	161

TABLES

1.1	Action planning reflective framework	6
2.1	Possible reasons for adopting a teaching practice	11
2.2	Introductory literature on learning and teaching	21
3.1	Conceptions of teaching	31
4.1	A planned approach to partnership working	61
4.2	HEA framework for student engagement through partnerships	64
7.1	High impact practices	101
10.1	Models of skills acquisition in the development of excellence	148
11.1	Examples of frameworks to support practice development	174
11.2	Your CPD Planner	182

Case Studies

2.1	No such thing as a 'Magic Weekend'	15
2.2	A real eye opener	17
2.3	Team teaching	18
2.4	Securing a teaching qualification	24
3.1	Blah blah blah	28
3.2	Making case study teaching really sing	32
3.3	Knowledge construction in Outdoor Education	36
3.4	Making a difference with Psychology	39
3.5	In praise of an Art School education or the impact of drawing out and leading forth	41
4.1	Leveraging student capital	47
4.2	Adding value through student learning about teaching	51
4.3	SMASH: Social Media for Academic Studies at Hallam	52
4.4	Student Active Engagement in Learning – the SAEL project	55
4.5	And Juno came too	58
4.6	A planned approach	61
5.1	This isn't working ...	68
5.2	The learning cycle	71
5.3	Getting the message across	74
5.4	Learning through lenses	77
5.5	'Can I observe your teaching?'	79
5.6	Don't lose the learning	82
6.1	Developing the specialist team	87
6.2	See the world as others see it	92
6.3	Engaging colleagues in a development	95
6.4	Engaging the entire work community	97

CASE STUDIES

7.1	Using student feedback to inform future practice	107
7.2	It worked!	109
8.1	Death by PowerPoint	119
8.2	First steps into research	122
8.3	Going the extra mile with a postgraduate teaching qualification	124
9.1	'I am titanium': an anthem for new course development	134
9.2	How the team of teachers ran	137
9.3	Helping postgraduate tutors to become skilled and confident teachers	141
9.4	Balancing my workload	143
10.1	How do I know?	150
10.2	Developing excellence together	158
10.3	Cultural glue	160
10.4	'Education can change the world'	162
11.1	My first mentor	172
11.2	We started a journal (!)	179
12.1	Heading for a showdown?	188

Acknowledgements

We are grateful to Sarah Tuckwell and staff at Routledge for their roles in bringing this book to publication, and also to our Series Editor Kate Exley for her vision behind the series and this new edition.

This book benefits significantly from the case studies and the extended think piece. We are thus particularly grateful to all those who have contributed in this way, and to the students who feature in them. We are also grateful to those who have helped us to develop the thinking behind different parts of the book, including David Laurence, Vivienne Bozalek and Brenda Leibowitz.

Many thanks, finally, to the colleagues, friends and family who have been inspirational, supportive and encouraging in equal measure; and particular thanks from Lorraine to Fraser and the special writing place.

Series editor introduction

THE SERIES

The Key Guides for Effective Teaching in Higher Education were initially discussed as an idea in 2002, and the first group of four titles were published in 2004. New titles have continued to be added and the Series now boasts twelve books (with new titles and further new editions of some of the older volumes in the pipeline).

It has always been intended that the books would be primarily of use to new teachers in universities and colleges. It has been exciting to see them being used to support postgraduate certificate programmes in teaching and learning for new academic staff and clinical teachers, and also the skills training programmes for post-graduate students who are beginning to teach. A less anticipated, but very valued, readership has been the experienced teachers who have dipped into the books when reviewing their teaching or referenced them when making claims for teaching recognition or promotion. Authors are very grateful to these colleagues who have given constructive feedback and made further suggestions on teaching approaches and shared examples of their practice all of which has fed-forward into later editions of titles.

In the UK, the work of the Higher Education Academy (HEA), now part of Advance HE, in developing a Professional Standards Framework (UKPSF), on behalf of the sector, has also raised the importance of providing good quality guidance and support for those beginning their teaching careers. It is therefore intended that the series would also provide a useful set of sources for those seeking to gain professional recognition for their practice against the UKPSF.

SERIES EDITOR INTRODUCTION

KEY THEMES OF THE SERIES

The books are all attempting to combine two things: to be very practical and provide lots of examples of methods and techniques, and also to link to educational theory and underpinning research. Articles are referenced, further readings are suggested and researchers in the field are quoted. There is also much enthusiasm here to link to the wide range of teaching development activities thriving in the disciplines, supported by the small grant schemes and conferences provided by Advance HE, Society for Research in Higher Education, Professional bodies etc. The need to tailor teaching approaches to meet the demands of different subject areas and to provide new teachers with examples of practice that are easily recognisable in their fields of study is seen as being very important by all the series authors. To this end the books include many examples drawn from a wide range of academic subjects and different kinds of Higher Education institutions. This theme of diversity is also embraced when considering the heterogeneous groups of students we now teach and the colleagues we work alongside. Students and teachers alike include people of different age, experience, knowledge, skills, culture, language, etc., and all the books include discussion of the issues and demands this places on teachers and learners in today's universities.

In the series as a whole there is also more than half an eye trying to peer into the future – what will teaching and learning look like in 10 or 20 years' time? How will student expectations, government policy, funding streams, and new technological advances and legislation affect what happens in our learning spaces of the future? What impact will this have on the way teaching is led and managed in institutions? You will see, therefore, that many of the books do include chapters that aim to look ahead and tap into the thinking of our most innovative and creative teachers and teaching leaders in an attempt to crystal-ball gaze. So these were the original ideas underpinning the series, and my co-authors and I have tried hard to keep them in mind as we researched our topics and typed away. We really hope that you find the books to be useful and interesting, whether you are a new teacher just starting out in your teaching career, or you are an experienced teacher reflecting on your practice and reviewing what you do.

DEVELOPING YOUR TEACHING, SECOND EDITION

Peter Kahn and Lorraine Anderson have taken a fresh look at the ways we can seek to develop our teaching since the first edition of this book was

SERIES EDITOR INTRODUCTION

published in 2006. They reflect on the changing landscape of Higher Education and have produced a radically updated and re-structured second edition. It retains however, all that was praised in the original and is an accessible and well-written work. It provides a beautiful blend of practical and usable development strategies for new and experienced teachers to employ, with a strong theoretical underpinning and it is very clear that the authors possess a grounded knowledge of 'just how it is' in Higher Education.

Kate Exley
Series Editor

Chapter 1

Introduction: The teaching landscape

INTRODUCTION

What is it that helps someone to become an excellent teacher? What enables you to take your teaching to a new level? Essentially, what are the influences, approaches and actions that you need to consider or adopt in order to help you to *develop* your teaching? The aim in this book is not to present an end point or an ideal vision to which you might aspire but to explore a number of questions and to consider a range of responses, in order to stimulate your thinking about what might work for you in your professional context. We will explore the process of developing your teaching with the help of a number of colleagues, from a range of discipline backgrounds and from across the sector, through their case studies and personal reflections; and in one example through an extended thinkpiece on the concept of excellence in teaching. These approaches will help you to examine your practice though a number of lenses and support you to begin – and hopefully encourage you to continue – a process of self-evaluation on your practice; viewing it always as a 'work in progress' rather than the finished article. In a nutshell, this book is for everyone who would like to think more deeply about their teaching, for those who would like to enhance their practice, and to enable all of us to continue to develop as professionals.

We all need to be inspired, enthused and motivated to develop our practice. So, before we begin to look at what this book can offer you, take a few minutes to think about what you can offer yourself. Think about the following question and consider what your response tells you about your identity as a teacher in higher education and your approach to developing your practice.

INTRODUCTION: THE TEACHING LANDSCAPE

My attitude to developing my teaching has been to:

(a) do enough to get by
(b) look for inspiration from others
(c) attend staff development workshops
(d) seek excellence

Do you grasp every development opportunity with both hands or do you wait to be prompted by others to engage with the idea of improving your practice? Are you the kind of person who wants to continue to grow and develop as a person and as a professional or are you happy feeling that you are doing 'just enough'? Are you content to be this kind of person? This kind of professional? By choosing to read this book do you want make a change to your approach?

In a time where constant change has become the new normal this may sound worthy – but exhausting. The tertiary education system is also an area where adopting a positive and thoughtful approach towards your teaching may be viewed as an ambiguous career move in a climate apparently ruled both politically and economically by the demands of the research assessment exercise and the pressures to publish; and to keep on publishing. We need to be able to find the motivation to help us to maintain our currency and to retain our enthusiasm as learners ourselves. Maureen Andrade, from Utah Valley University, shares with us some insights into how she has achieved this.

> The development of my teaching has been motivated by autonomy, mastery, and purpose (Pink, 2009). I thrive on autonomy to make decisions about what and how I teach. I seek mastery of my content and embrace opportunities to continue to learn through professional development, including my own scholarly contributions, and I am driven by purpose—helping learners fulfil their goals and sharing what I know with others. I have recently implemented the following new elements in my teaching:
>
> ■ a team e-portfolio assignment in both an online and a face-to-face class
> ■ feedback using a screencast video tool
> ■ an online quiz game in class, where students participated using their smartphones, to help learners build foundational knowledge of concepts prior to application

INTRODUCTION: THE TEACHING LANDSCAPE

- a website for class documents that students can access for in-class activities. A paperless environment!

I didn't even dream of these activities 25 years ago. These approaches may not be new to others, but they were new to me. The answer to what helps one develop one's teaching is partly motivation and partly the nature of teaching. Teaching involves the constant disruption of one's practice.

Autonomy: not all of us have as much of this as we might like. On occasion we may be asked to teach someone else's class and to have to use their material. Or we may find ourselves part of a team whose approach doesn't quite gel with our own. And even if we do have some flexibility in *what* we do, we are often restricted by the teaching accommodation that we're allocated as to *where* we are required to do it! Working at ways to create an element of autonomy is however, essential to us developing and being able to realise our own personal philosophy of teaching and to expand and enhance our practice.

In **Chapter 2** we look at how we can go about exercising that autonomy by choosing effective approaches in our teaching. To what extent do we use our own personal experience as learners and how much do we base our practice on what we see around us, whether that's colleagues in action, relevant literature or conferences? In **Chapter 3** we look at the disciplinary influences that can play a significant role here and the ways of working that they involve. These 'signature pedagogies' can influence the acceptance or uptake of new approaches by our colleagues, while students may often not see the inherent benefit of some teaching and learning activities until later in their academic or professional career, if the activity takes them out of their comfort zone at that time. This can lead to pressures for us to think that there is one 'right' way to teach, in the same way that students can take a surface or strategic approach to their learning in looking for the 'right' answer as opposed to engaging with a reflective learning process.

And what is it that our students are telling us? In the current teaching landscape, the idea of the 'student voice' is a very powerful concept and it plays a central role in a student-centred approach to developing one's teaching. Yet, whilst making for a good pedagogical approach, when coupled with the current focus on student fees and rising costs it can be distorted into a way of viewing students primarily as customers, rather than learners. Do students think this way too? Based on an online survey of over 1,000 full and part-time undergraduates in the UK (UUK,

INTRODUCTION: THE TEACHING LANDSCAPE

2017) Universities UK reported that slightly less than half (47 per cent) of the undergraduate students surveyed saw themselves as customers of their university. While this is a significant figure the report also concluded that although 'being a consumer is clearly an important part of being a student, it does not appear to be the overriding feature' (UUK, 2017: 5). Positioning teachers and students in a consumer-based relationship has potential implications for how we teach and how our students learn. 'When lecturers think of students as customers, it influences how they teach . . . Fear of bad teaching evaluations from students influences the extent to which lecturers challenge them' (Matthews, 2018).

As we develop our teaching we also need to work at developing the kinds of relationships we have with our students, and the purpose they serve.

> Universities that care about learning . . . value an educational culture in which the student-lecturer relationship is at the heart of teaching and learning. Staff at these universities tend to do more than talk at, about, or survey students, they talk *with* them.
>
> (Matthews, 2018)

Across the teaching landscape, learning conversations are being re-framed and alternative narratives proposed. **Chapter 4** looks at one of the most compelling of these narratives: students as partners. Working in partnership with our students in learning and teaching can be viewed as a robust response 'to the all-too-common narrative of students as customers . . . and a chance for cultural change and a new way of "doing" higher education' (Matthews, 2018).

Lots of ideas then. However, when we begin to think about developing our practice there can appear to be many more questions than answers. Sometimes this is stimulating and motivating but it can also prove to be a turn off from development activities and you might feel that it is better to stick with tried and tested methods; if it ain't broke, don't fix it. Yet, as professional university teachers we have ownership of and responsibility for our professional development. Eraut (1987) identified four models which reflect the history of approaches and attitudes towards teacher professional development (see Figure 1.1).

The four models trace the movement from an individually focused, externally directed approach to development towards greater personal ownership of the development process, and associated collective focus on practice and practical application of learning. Neither teaching nor development does – or should – take place in a vacuum!

INTRODUCTION: THE TEACHING LANDSCAPE

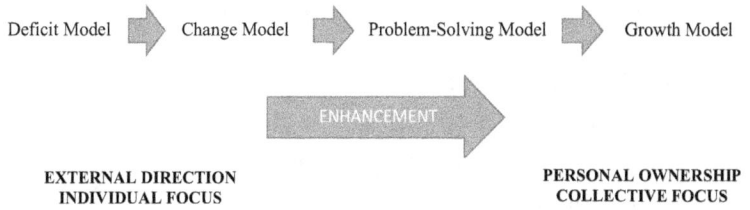

FIGURE 1.1 Models of teacher professional development, adapted from Eraut (1987)

The final stage, or growth model, facilitates ongoing professional development through processes such as inquiry and reflection. We explore the concepts of reflection and reflective practice in **Chapter 5** where you are encouraged to look at your teaching using a range of tools, including lenses on practice, involving your colleagues, and developing your own strategies to incorporate reflection into your work as a day-to-day activity. In many ways, reflection can be considered as giving yourself feedback – and most importantly feedforward – on your practice, in the same way that you do for students on their work. It provides you with the opportunity to evaluate your current position and to use that information to plan for your future development. You can use a structured framework of questions to guide you through the process of self-evaluation, reflection and action planning. The structured nature of the questions supports you in addressing all aspects of the planning as the sequence of questions follows on logically one from the other, without allowing you to avoid any potentially difficult or challenging aspects! Table 1.1 provides an example of what such a framework might look like. You might want to consider including other questions that are relevant to your specific context.

THE DISCIPLINE OF NOTICING

A good deal of richness and potential can come from learning derived directly from your teaching experience. Such emergent learning arises from your own practice in the course of your everyday activities, and is rooted in, drawn from, and based upon that experience. It comes from being more attuned to what Mason (2002) calls 'the discipline of noticing'. Knowledge about your teaching develops, is tested, reviewed, and refined through iterative cycles that lead to the emergence of deeper understanding. We should not restrict ourselves to just our own ideas,

INTRODUCTION: THE TEACHING LANDSCAPE

TABLE 1.1 Action planning reflective framework

What kind of teacher am I now?
What are my roles and responsibilities?
What does my personal philosophy of teaching look like?
What kind of teacher do I want to be?
Who are my role models?
What are my aspirations?
Where do I see myself in five years' time?
How will I get there?
What are my short term goals? And long term?
What resources are available to support me?
How can I access them?
What barriers exist to inhibit me from realising my goals?
How can I address these barriers?

however, and **Chapter 6** moves on to discuss how you might draw ideas from working with others and taking a more collective approach to practice. Eraut's (1994: 13) learning professional 'relies on three main sources: publications in a variety of media; practical experience; and *people*' (our emphasis). We invite you to engage with your colleagues in dialogue, debate and a more collaborative working approach to enhancing practice.

Much has changed in the higher education landscape since the first edition of *Developing your Teaching* was published. We now inhabit an academic environment that is fully digital, wholly global and undeniably complex with all that means in terms of pace of change and higher and more demanding expectations. One should, however, avoid adopting a passive and unreflective acceptance of these changes. In **Chapter 7** we look at drivers within our practice and encourage you to explore them, discuss and debate with colleagues, and subject them to critique. For example the increasing emphasis on teaching for graduate employability forms a significant driver – what does this mean for our practice in terms of disciplinary content? The inclusion of placements, internships and work-based learning opportunities? The moves to normalise enterprise and entrepreneurship as part of the curriculum?

INTRODUCTION: THE TEACHING LANDSCAPE

FLYING THE FLAG

In **Chapter 8** we encourage you to consider introducing new developments into your teaching and also to begin thinking about researching your teaching practice. Researching our own teaching can support our development in a number of ways, including the refining of professional judgement and skills, encouraging us to consider our academic practice from a holistic standpoint, and perhaps most importantly, providing us with greater insight into student learning. The scholarship of teaching and learning (SoTL) can provide a rich seam of learning in parallel to our discipline-based research. Part of this may involve stepping forward and 'flying the flag' for this approach in your department or school. In **Chapter 9** we consider the challenges and opportunities inherent in taking a lead within your teaching practice. Adopting such a role can prove to be exciting and rewarding but it is also worth reflecting on the proverb – 'The person who thinks he is leading but has no followers is merely taking a stroll.' Gaining support and confidence from your colleagues takes more than simply being appointed in a leadership position. Building positive and effective relationships is a key part of that process and links directly to the topics of several of the preceding chapters, including working with, and learning from, others through collective engagement.

REALISING EXCELLENCE – CONCEPT AND PRACTICE

Whether it be in teaching, SoTL or disciplinary-based research we all strive for excellence; and the expectation to attain excellence is all around us. But what does that actually mean? And what might it look like in your practice? In **Chapter 10** we consider the concept of excellence in teaching and reflect on how it might be realised. Being able to drive that excellent practice towards enhancing your career is something that we explore in **Chapter 11**, but rather than advocating that you take a linear approach, we encourage you to 'go wide' and engage with the concept of career-wide enhancement in both your practice and your career. You may find yourself stretched by some of the suggestions made here but having the *confidence* to develop is a key aspect of moving your practice on. Finally, **Chapter 12**, draws together the key components of our dialogue with you, the reader. It aims to support you in deciding upon the choices you will make over the direction of your development. Discovering what works for you and situating this within your own personal story is an important part of shaping the development of your teaching.

INTRODUCTION: THE TEACHING LANDSCAPE

CONCLUSIONS

Actively seeking out inspiration for your teaching can help you to view your teaching practice in a new light and from a fresh perspective. Real examples of the ways in which theoretical ideas, suggestions or strategies can work in practice are an excellent way in which to achieve this and can help you to gain insight into how those approaches might work for you in developing your teaching. In this book we aim to provide you with that inspiration through the inclusion of authentic case studies from practice. Each of the case studies has been provided by colleagues working currently in higher education. Their personal stories originate from a range of discipline areas and countries around the world, providing examples of development in action. Each individual example demonstrates a range of approaches to developing teaching such as addressing challenges, exploring issues through personal narratives, and adopting a variety of ways to develop practice. Use the case studies to gain insight into those ideas, activities or approaches. Use the review points to reflect on how they might work for you in developing your own practice and in seeking excellence.

Revisit your response to the initial question on your attitude to developing your teaching. Do you get ideas from team teaching or sharing experiences with colleagues? Perhaps you prefer to work on your own, seeking out articles or books for information and new ideas. Or maybe you teach in the way that you were taught, perhaps emulating a favourite lecturer or tutor, and you haven't considered making any changes to that approach. Yet, consider in that case, how will you be able to respond to the changing higher education system? How will you deal with the changing student population that has resulted from widening participation, internationalisation and inclusion strategies? Or the model of student as consumer; or as partner? And how will you fit within an education system geared to rapid technological advance, inter-professional working and innovation? In our professional practice, learning and development are integral parts of all of the roles we play as both teachers and researchers; and also as scholars. For Boyer (1990: 16), this idea of scholarship is not only 'engaging in original research' but 'also stepping back from one's investigation, looking for connections, building bridges between theory and practice, and communicating one's knowledge effectively': a holistic approach to our practice, within which teaching forms an integral part. All of this sits, of course, within the wider landscape of teaching in higher education.

REFERENCES

Boyer, E. L. (1990). *Scholarship Reconsidered: Priorities of the Professoriate*. San Francisco: Carnegie Foundation/Jossey-Bass.

Eraut, M. (1987). Inservice teacher education. In M. Dunkin (ed.), *The International Encyclopedia of Teaching and Teacher Education*. New York: Pergamon Press.

Eraut, M. (1994). *Developing Professional Knowledge and Competence*. London: Falmer Press.

Mason, J. (2002). *Researching Your Own Practice*: The Discipline of Noticing. London: RoutledgeFalmer.

Matthews (2018). Stop treating students as customers and work with them as partners in learning. *The Conversation*, 12 April 2018. https://theconversation.com/stop-treating-students-like-customers-and-start-working-with-them-as-partners-in-learning-93276 [Online, accessed 16 September 2018].

Pink, D. (2009). *Drive*. New York: Riverhead Books.

Universities UK (UUK) (2017). Around a half of students now see themselves as customers of their university – new ComRes survey, 21 June 2017. www.universitiesuk.ac.uk/news/Pages/Around-a-half-of-students-now-see-themselves-as-customers-of-their-university.aspx [Online, accessed 16 September 2018].

Universities UK (UUK) (2017). *Education, Consumer Rights and Maintaining Trust: What students want from their university*. London: UUK. www.universitiesuk.ac.uk/policy-and-analysis/reports/Documents/2017/education-consumer-rights-maintaining-trust-web.pdf [Online, accessed 16 September 2018].

Chapter 2

Choosing effective teaching practices

INTRODUCTION

If you are running a teaching session, how do you start it? Perhaps you dive straight in to make your first point, or maybe you begin with a statement of the learning outcomes you expect the students will have achieved by the end of the session. Which of these approaches is more effective? This chapter primarily looks at what it takes to justify your choices. You are unlikely to see any detailed operating procedures for required activity in a lecture hall!

One thing, however, is clear – the evidence for any preferred practice will not just fall into your lap. So the chapter also looks at realistic strategies to access the information that you require, as well as highlighting triggers that will prompt you to find evidence. After all, there are so many variables at play in education that your personal context is highly relevant to how you teach. We do assume that you have at least some scope to determine which teaching practices you will employ. You may not have the freedom to choose whether to see students individually or in a large group, but you would usually have the scope to choose how to start a teaching session.

EVIDENCE FROM EXPERIENCE

What does your own experience indicate is an effective way to start, say, a lecture? We will use this example of starting a lecture to illustrate our discussion of what makes for a suitable teaching practice. You will have a store of your own memories as a student and as a teacher on which to draw. Perhaps you once tried to start a lecture by reading out a list of learning outcomes – and found a sea of bemused faces. You will have seen things that work and you will have noticed practices you want to avoid.

How good, though, is the evidence that stems from this experience? Perhaps you recited your list of outcomes while the students were half asleep or preoccupied with an examination. The clear lesson is that you may well need to explore why something works or does not work. Unless you articulate and analyse the implications of your experience it may well be difficult to ascertain whether it is evidence or prejudice; an issue we shall explore further in Chapter 4.

So what kinds of reasons do teachers propose to justify their practice? Table 2.1 summarises a range of reasons. Consider a particular teaching practice that you employ and see how many of these reasons in the table apply.

TABLE 2.1 Possible reasons for adopting a teaching practice

Category	Reasons for adopting a practice
Personal	■ This has worked for me in the past. ■ I am interested in taking this on. ■ I'm comfortable teaching in this fashion. ■ I found it helpful when I was a student. ■ This aligns with my personal approach to teaching.
Student	■ Students say that they like it this way. ■ Students learn effectively, and receive good grades. ■ Students were able to complete the required tasks. ■ I am able to address a wide range of learning outcomes. ■ I receive positive feedback from the students. ■ This leads to good relationships with the students. ■ The students get involved and ask perceptive questions. ■ Students choose my question on the examination above other questions.
Professional	■ The resources (technology, technicians, materials, etc.) are in place. ■ I have time for this approach. ■ This fits with the pattern of teaching in my department/discipline. ■ I am allowed to do this. ■ I am obliged to use this method ■ The process is efficient. ■ Colleagues tell me they like it.

CHOOSING EFFECTIVE TEACHING PRACTICES

In many respects it is easy to make a case for the way that you teach; you simply select several reasons that appeal to you or support what you want to do. But why have you neglected so many other factors? Why have you accorded such weight to these particular reasons? Is it really the case that each of your reasons actually applies? Without explicitly addressing these concerns it would be rash to say that you had created a more genuine rational justification for adopting any particular practice. Nietzsche, certainly, was aware that our claims to rationality often simply reflect our own subjective choices, rather than anything more objective.

Consider, for instance, the edited extract below from an assignment on a course in learning and teaching. The lecturer is seeking to justify her particular use of lectures that involve interaction with students. She cites her own experience, both as a student and lecturer, as evidence for the

---

Box 2.1
JUSTIFICATION OF A LECTURER'S PRACTICE

It has not been long since I was a student myself. Therefore I have some insight into how students feel about long lectures in which the lecturer talks and they have to listen for the whole time. I will ensure my lectures are interactive, by using case studies and class exercises to generate interesting discussions. This will allow the students to learn through being involved rather than just by listening. As a result the student will develop critical thinking skills, a key outcome for the knowledge economy. Moreover a prerequisite of admission onto the programme is that students have a minimum of two years' work experience. They will thus have real world examples of the issues, making their input useful. However, from past experience I know that this is easier said than done. In previous lectures I have given it has been very difficult to get some students to participate. Although I have used class exercises, group work and working in pairs, it had been difficult to get all students to participate without starting to embarrass them by calling out their names, a technique I was not willing to use. Therefore, what usually happens is that some students participate while others do not. This can be attributed to cultural reasons, in that some of my students may come from cultures that view the lecture as a 'teaching' venue in which the learner should not participate. This is difficult to change in a few weeks.

proposed practices, and proposes that involvement in one's own learning is important if one is to develop higher-level skills. She considers one strategy that she might have employed, and dismisses this.

There are a number of issues that would need to be addressed if one were to improve the rational basis for the practice she describes. Perhaps there are other strategies she could have considered which would not have involved forcing students to contribute.

- Introduce some individual exercises to prepare the students for the group or pair activities.
- Discuss some of the cultural issues openly with the students. (Although she does recognise the practical difficulties of shifting cultural expectations in a short space of time.)
- Draw directly on the work experience that each student had undergone, and use this as a basis for encouraging students to contribute.

Does she effectively accept a teaching situation in which only some students will be able to attain these desired higher-level skills? She might have argued that even where not all students directly contribute, all students could still attain the higher-level skills as a result of the richer environment. Perhaps she could have explicitly ensured that the different contributions highlighted different viewpoints, emphasising the need for criticality. This would require an appreciation that more is required than simple 'involvement' for students to learn, even if this is seen as important. Addressing these sorts of fundamental questions could, indeed, provide a way to take one's teaching to a new level – to an excellent standard.

In providing a more robust justification for your approach, you may find that certain aspects of the given practice are not as carefully thought out as you had initially imagined, and perhaps this will lead you to adapt the practice somewhat. An analysis of your own attempt to recite a list of learning outcomes might lead you to realise that a distracted student could easily miss out. This might lead you to put the outcomes onto a PowerPoint slide or visualiser, and to leave it up for a few seconds. Such practices, of course, might be a more rational approach in light of your experience, but we have yet to see if they are effective! This next review point encourages you to put one of your own teaching practices under the microscope. (You might not actually carry out the review as proposed here, but it could nonetheless usefully inform an assignment on a teaching qualification).

CHOOSING EFFECTIVE TEACHING PRACTICES

> **Review point 2.1**
> **A RATIONALE FOR PRACTICE**
>
> 1. Select any practice that you carry out in your teaching and write half a page on why you carry out the practice in the way that you do (or select a short piece of writing where you have already provided a rationale for some aspect of your teaching).
>
> 2. Strengthen your rationale in the following ways:
>   - Underline each reason that you have advanced for employing the practice.
>   - Provide additional statements to support each reason.
>   - Provide further reasons to support your practice (looking at Table 2.1 may help to generate ideas for further reasons).
>   - Identify any reasons why you might not employ the practice, and provide a counter argument to discount each reason.

You might also want to construct a case for adopting an alternative practice, perhaps one you have heard exists but of which you have no direct experience. It is, however, more difficult to construct a case for a method of teaching that you have little experience of using. How do you even find out what the alternatives actually are? It is unrealistic to expect you to invent practical alternatives on the spot. Reasons for adopting something different may simply not occur to you. It is easy to dismiss any reasons that do come to mind. But only when you can realistically see what the alternatives actually involve are you in a position to begin to see which practice is likely to be more effective. And yet it may well be that another practice would be far better for you, your students and your context.

One option is to gain a wider range of experience. You could experiment with different ways of starting a lecture, and see what seems to work. Another alternative is to undertake experiences that help you to re-frame the way that you see teaching and learning. Mo Andrew in the case study that follows found two sources for this. One of the main reasons to take a teaching qualification is to widen your repertoire of teaching methods, but it will give you further insight into what it means to be a student.

Case study 2.1
NO SUCH THING AS A 'MAGIC WEEKEND'

Mo Andrew, Employability and Opportunities, Edinburgh Napier University

I entered teaching in Higher Education (HE) from a people development background within a nationwide business where employee development was historically grounded in the promotional-ladder framework, with no tangible development actually being provided to climb this ladder successfully. However, business practice changed through a deepening understanding that becoming a leader did not happen overnight and without appropriate support. It was acknowledged that our newly appointed leaders were being expected to leave their team role on Friday and pass through what was glibly referred to as a 'magic weekend'. They commenced their new leadership role the following Monday being expected to know how to lead, motivate and develop their people.

How, you may ask, does this relate to the development of my HE teaching practice? It was the start of some radical but fundamental adjustment to my perception of successful people development. It was also the springboard towards appreciating that likewise there is no 'magic weekend' for a new graduate in their first graduate role. When commencing my teaching role I realised my practice must develop specifically for HE if I were to become truly effective in helping students develop personal and professional attributes to support their graduate career.

I also recognised that a deeper understanding of the student perspective and development of some effective partnerships with students would be the most effective way to support my teaching aspirations. Two significant experiences were particularly essential with this:

1. Becoming a student myself; enrolling in a part-time online MSc programme in Blended and Online Education at Edinburgh Napier University. This not only encouraged me to reflect on my teaching methods and approaches but also provided some very valuable lessons, the most significant stemming from actually being a student myself. Consequently, I became better equipped to understand student learning expectations and developed teaching practices that widened the reach and depth of learning opportunities I offered. I acknowledged that I should be providing more diverse and personalised learning choices for students including: self-directed online learning,

video-shorts explaining theory (linked to 'flipped learning' practices), interactive webinars, and participation in online discussion.
2. As I personally immersed myself for the first time in HE learning I understood that what had been missing was the influence of open and honest student perspectives on my teaching practice. Fortuitously I was offered the opportunity to participate in the award-winning institutional initiative: 'Students as Colleagues' and I jumped at the chance to expand my new thirst for knowledge and critical assessment. Fortunately for me, my student colleague turned out to be an extremely bright, innovative and future-thinking Applied Sciences student who was unafraid and confident in providing assessment and feedback on my teaching practice, along with an additional student perspective. Her suggestions supported me in overcoming some personal and departmental assumptions about student learning choices, and she offered ideas that I may never have thought about on my own.

My combined learning within the MSc programme and participation in the 'Students as Colleagues' initiative encouraged me to develop more imaginative, innovative, succinct, and twenty-first-century learning approaches to teaching. Learning from these different perspectives stimulated development of alternative teaching methods e.g. instead of continuing to deliver three separate 2-hour workshops for a large student cohort, I designed one 1½-hour interactive lecture utilising activities suitable for a large raked theatre space; e.g. using videos, quizzes and small group exercises. This not only supported a reduction in teaching time from 6 hours to 1½ hours, whilst still providing desired learning that supported student's academic learning outcomes, it also met with approval and endorsement from my student colleague and her cohort.

I was able to include these experiences in my evidence towards successful application for Fellowship of the Higher Education Academy and believe that by continuing to seek out and nurture partnerships with students I will be in a stronger position to dispel any prospect of the 'Magic Weekend' experience as I continue to provide a variety of opportunities for developing essential skills and attributes for graduate life.

The final word on 'magic' comes from my student colleague whose feedback on our partnership included this quote: *"For me it [the partnership] was like seeing the other side of a magical mirror which you never get to see normally"* and we both agree that our continued partnership, and my new teaching qualification, brings benefit to: our relationship, the wider student community, and ultimately the university.

CHOOSING EFFECTIVE TEACHING PRACTICES

DRAWING IDEAS FROM OTHERS

The rapid pace of change in higher education can, though, make it difficult to respond to all the challenges that are thrown at us simply on the basis of our own experience. What better way than actually to draw on the experience of your colleagues? Many teaching qualifications include a requirement for you to observe colleagues teach. Such observations can have a profound impact, as Martin Twiste describes in the next case study.

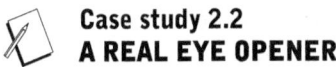

Case study 2.2
A REAL EYE OPENER

Martin Twiste, Directorate of Prosthetics and Orthotics, University of Salford

Having acquired my new post as a lecturer, I decided to become further educated myself. I enrolled on a programme that led to a Postgraduate Certificate in Higher Education Practice and Research. This, I thought, would help me in addressing the issues I had with my own teaching, so that I could better support my students in their learning. Part of the programme was based on teaching observations, and I found out that I was required to take part in five of these! For two of the observations I had to observe both my mentor and a peer on the programme. For the other three, my mentor, a peer, and another teacher of my choice had to observe me. The way I felt about my teaching was that I very much enjoyed giving lectures and found it satisfying when at least some students appeared to understand the material I was trying to get across. Unfortunately, this was probably not the case for the majority of students I was supposed to be educating. So I looked forward to seeing what others did in their teaching practice.

What surprised me most was that none of the lecturers I observed used the 'traditional' approach to lecturing of talking continuously for the full lecture period – which was what I had always done so far. Instead, they used a much more interactive approach, engaging the students from start to finish. This also appeared to support the students in learning far more effectively than they appeared to do in my lectures. Not surprisingly, after the three lecturers observed me, they were under the impression that the students switched off very early on in my lecture and consequently did not learn very much! Having reflected upon the teaching observations, I decided to implement a much more interactive teaching style within my own practice. This was an astonishing experience, as I soon noticed how much more interested the students were in what I was saying, and how much better they retained the information I presented. This approach to teaching was a real eye opener for me, and a reflection of the value of having taken part in the teaching observations.

Conversations with colleagues also offer a window onto their experience, say over a coffee. If someone in a similar situation to yourself has tried something and found that it proved to be effective in their practice, it may be relatively easy for you to try it out for yourself. Perhaps a colleague has found that it works really well to start a lecture with a captivating anecdote that follows on from the last lecture – some disciplines lend themselves well to this type of approach. Another colleague may begin by addressing a question that they raised at the end of the last session, asking if any students are able to shed light on it.

But conversations around teaching don't appear out of thin air. Someone needs to start them. Why not you? Share a problem or an innovation with a colleague who is interested in their teaching. You will soon learn which colleagues are ready to engage with you.

Team teaching offers extensive possibilities for these exchanges. In Case study 2.3 Martyn Stewart describes the impact on his teaching that came from teaching with colleagues. One advantage of such professional interactions is that there is usually scope to address why a practice might be effective in any given context. Your colleague might have indicated that they want their students to become actively involved in any lecture that they give – but that this only works in their experience if the students become interested in the material. Hence their immediate concern is to engage the interest of the students before encouraging student participation; and so perhaps they always begin classes with a compelling problem.

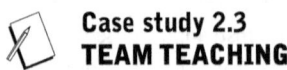

Case study 2.3
TEAM TEACHING

Dr Martyn Stewart, Education and Training, Liverpool School of Tropical Medicine (formely School of Biological and Earth Science, Liverpool John Moores University).

Fieldwork is a highly compact learning environment – effectively a module-worth of teaching and learning in a week – and this compactness is ideal for unpicking what works well in terms of timing and sequencing of learning activities. This case study describes how one particular trip had a marked impact in my understanding of what constituted effective teaching.

The majority of field trips centre around field lectures interspersed with part-day activities where students practise skills at new sites each day. This usually works well. However, in Earth Sciences, learning how to construct a geological map is quite a challenging task, requiring an understanding of landscape, rock identification and building a 3-D model of the underground strata.

One particular mapping trip I attended (as a teaching assistant) was structured quite differently. Instead of moving from site to site, the trip consisted of ten days based at the same location which had a complex range of geological features. Early days of the trip consisted of no more than an hour of lecture to introduce new skills, but from then on and for the bulk of the ten days students were simply let go to work in teams to build up the map for themselves, with staff wandering around to provide guidance and feedback. The students certainly struggled during the early stages, but they were aware they had the luxury of time to develop their understandings and go through the process of discovering things for themselves rather than just 'wait for the lecturers to explain what's going on'.

Initially I considered this trip lacking structure, scope and variety compared to previously attended trips planned as teacher-led mapping 'tours'. The key turning point here was the realisation that *this* was what mapping is actually like. It isn't easy, it takes time and one has to develop these skills over time by getting immersed in the task. Cramming as many sites in as possible doesn't matter. And it worked – the quality of the students' work was extremely high as was their confidence in their mapping capabilities as they advanced onto their field-based research projects.

This for me was the point at which I began to reflect on what the term student-centred learning *really* meant – recognising the importance of letting go and especially creating space in any programme to enable enquiry-driven learning – I recall myself learning to map properly on independent fieldwork, rather than from listening to my teachers. It also sparked my understanding of appropriately aligning learning activities to intended learning outcomes. The skills to build a geological map are, by nature, exploratory and constructive. Therefore the activity has to be structured to allow the student to experience this. The legacy of this is that I now put great effort and thought into how I design new learning activities, and how the students engage with their learning, rather than 'what I shall teach'.

THE WRITTEN WORD

Discussions with colleagues can open up a wide range of experience to you, and yet practice is often articulated in written form. Case studies, practical texts on a given area of teaching, and so on typically provide descriptions of practice and may give a rationale as to why the practices are appropriate. For instance, Yeo, Edwards, Smith and Webb (2001) describe a situation where the students on a lecture course on legal studies had become confused about what they should be learning. The course was trying to cover too much. The lecturer responded by refocusing on the learning outcomes; cutting out material that was less important, distributing handouts that informed the students of the outcomes of each particular lecture, along with an outline of the lecture. This enabled the students to realise that the lecturer wanted them to appreciate different approaches to criminal law, rather than simply adopt a single method.

The written word does have an advantage in that you will be able to cite your source relatively easily in the assignments on your teaching qualification. Case studies are becoming increasingly available, whether on institutional repositories (check out those available within your own institution) or across the internet (as provided, for instance, on the website of the organisation Advance HE). Practical texts on teaching and learning are another point of departure, with some popular books highlighted in Table 2.2.

GAINING FROM RESEARCH

Some descriptions of practice incorporate or rely on formal evaluation – and it is here that we move to a deeper level of rigour in our search for what works in higher education. Your own experience, contributions from colleagues and descriptions of practice are all at a relatively informal level. It can be hard to tell if one practice genuinely results in an improvement over another practice. Evaluation is important because it helps to provide a more considered understanding as to *why* the practice was effective. For instance, in the case study from Yeo et al. (2001) evaluation indicated that the changes made significant difference to the student experience on the course, as the students' concerns had been addressed more directly. As people develop systematic and reasoned understandings of why a teaching practice is effective we arrive at educational theory. Such theory is notorious amongst staff in higher education for its jargon and apparent lack of relevance to the day-to-day work of a lecturer.

TABLE 2.2 Introductory literature on learning and teaching

Focus of practice	Suggested text(s)
General	*A Handbook for Learning and Teaching in Higher Education* (Fry, Ketteridge, & Marshall, 2015); *Reflective Teaching in Higher Education* (Ashwin, Boud, Coate, Hallett, & Keane, 2015); *Rethinking University Teaching* (Laurillard, 2013); *Teaching for Quality Learning at University* (Biggs & Tang, 2011); *The Lecturer's Toolkit* (Race, 2014)
Specific areas of teaching and supporting learning	Key guides for effective teaching in higher education (from Routledge), of which this book is one example; *Learning in Groups* (Jaques & Salmon, 2007); *Creating Significant Learning Experiences* (Fink, 2013)
Assessment	*Assessment for learning* (Black, Harrison, Lee, Marshall, & William, 2003); *Classroom Assessment Techniques* (Angelo & Cross, 2005)
Subject specific literature	Titles in the series from Routledge 'Effective Learning and Teaching in Higher Education', with each text focusing on a specific discipline.

Nonetheless, it is hard to imagine a Master's level qualification in any profession or discipline that dismisses theory out of hand! Theory enables one to move beyond piling up reasons to justify a practice.

Theory is particularly useful when framing an innovation – we need not proceed simply on the basis of trial and error. Of course, some theories are more far reaching than others, providing a sound basis for a wider range of innovations. Jarvis (2012) and Schunk (2012) both provide a good introduction to a range of learning theories. The most widely employed theory of learning, in broad terms at least, is that of constructivism. Learning is seen to entail a student creating constructs in their own mind, as a result of processes that are personal to them as a learner. Cognitive processes, for instance, will involve the learner's direction of their own thinking. Some variants place a particular emphasis on the role that social interaction plays in the construction of understanding.

Perhaps your teaching qualification has suggested that starting with a statement of the learning outcomes to be addressed in the lecture is a good way to begin. In our case, a search within the British Educational

Index with the words 'learning outcomes' yielded two highly cited studies that caught the eye. Hussey and Smith (2002) claimed that

> Learning outcomes have value when properly conceived and used in ways that respect their limitations and exploit their virtues, but they are damaging to education if seen as precise prescriptions that must be spelled out in detail before teaching can begin and which are objective and measurable devices suitable for monitoring educational practices.
>
> (p. 222)

Hussey and Smith (2003), meanwhile, go on to argue that teaching requires a careful balance between a lecturer's intentions for student learning and the contributions that students themselves make; and that being too upfront about the outcomes of an individual session could upset that balance. These studies by Hussey and Smith are broadly located within a paradigm of learning that is grounded in constructivism.

If you are about to plan your teaching for the next term or semester or are about to design a course unit, though, you may wish to consider doing so in light of a more specific theory. An assignment on a programme in learning and teaching that requires you to justify your practice would also provide a suitable opportunity to test the relevance of a specific theory. Unless you actually work with a theory in the context of your practice you are unlikely to be able to ascertain its usefulness.

Take, for instance, the theory of critical pedagogy (Freire, 2014). This theory suggests that teaching and learning should be framed by the aspirations, needs and backgrounds of students. Critical programmes of education integrate dialogue between students and teachers, especially in relation to the uses to which their learning might be put. Part of the point is to understand the biases and assumptions that frame life in one's social setting, so that the status quo can then be challenged. If you were drawing on this theory to support your teaching, you might well want to start a teaching session as you mean to go on, with dialogue. In this case you might expect the learning outcomes themselves to be framed in a way that respects the sort of learning that emerges from a dialogue rather than from a monologue. All curricular decisions would be based on the needs and interests of the students involved, and choices as to what would be studied, and how, would be made jointly by teachers and students. This approach is designed to transform teaching into a form of social activism, although its perspectives can be applied without seeking to foment a revolution! Are there aspects of the disciplinary or professional setting

CHOOSING EFFECTIVE TEACHING PRACTICES

in which your students are operating that might warrant change? The perspectives of critical pedagogy are easier to introduce in some settings than others, but that is something that is true for all educational theory.

The manner in which you engage with theory does make a difference. A straightforward summary of a theory doesn't always provide sufficient insight for you actually to adapt your own teaching in your own unique circumstances. If your interest is in going beyond the standard approaches used in your own department or if you are looking to gain a distinction on a Master's level teaching qualification (one clear form of excellence), then you will want to access research studies directly or a join a network of colleagues also interested in that approach (something that would be key for critical pedagogy). Each of us works in a given institutional and disciplinary context, with specific students and colleagues who respond in their own unique ways to education. A thorough understanding of an educational theory, one that appreciates its limitations as well as its strengths, can only come from a more substantive engagement with research literature. Clearly this involves additional time – but the extra effort may be worthwhile when developing initial expertise, designing a new course or spearheading an innovation.

Review point 2.2
A COMPARISON

1. Develop a rationale for an alternative practice to the one that you described above on page 14. Incorporate reasons into your rationale that relate to your own experience; practical literature; one specific theory.

2. Which rationale do you find more convincing? The rationale created during the earlier review point, or the rationale for this activity?

CONCLUSION: BEYOND WHAT IS RATIONAL

The capacity to justify your choice of teaching practices is an essential part of most qualifications in higher education teaching. In years gone by gaining a teaching qualification may have seemed an imposition. It was the duty of students to learn, and the duty of the lecturer to, well, lecture.

The evolving landscape of higher education that we saw in the previous chapter, though, means that the ultimate focus is now on student learning rather than staff lecturing. Even if you realise that a course on teaching is a standard expectation of your working context, though, this won't necessarily energise your engagement with something that you haven't straightforwardly chosen to undertake. We see in the case study that follows from Susanne Goetzold that something shifted for her after that sinking feeling she experienced on being 'invited' to join a Postgraduate Certificate in Learning, Teaching and Assessment Practice. The difference came when she had the opportunity to explore a genuinely intriguing issue in her teaching, taking her beyond ticking the box. Ultimately, a fully convincing justification for your practice only comes with a wholehearted readiness to developing your teaching.

Case study 2.4
SECURING A TEACHING QUALIFICATION

Susanne Goetzold, School of Health and Social Care, Edinburgh Napier University

I clearly remember a PhD being mentioned as part of my Continuing Professional Development when I applied for my first lecturing post. Mention of the Postgraduate Certificate in Learning Teaching and Assessment Practice in Higher Education is rather vague in my memory. Enthusiasm was therefore a little limited when the invitation to enrol dropped into my inbox. It was the support from the team teaching the certificate, along with an almost universal sense of 'shared pain' from those who had trodden this path before, which helped me throughout the year.

Studying while also working full time was difficult, but it is the situation most of my students find themselves in, as they commit to online study towards an advanced practice award. I certainly had to rehearse my juggling skills again in an attempt to find sufficient time for the reading. This was the first time I was working towards a qualification I had not chosen by interest and that certainly impacted on motivation in the early stages, as I was trying to get my head round new vocabulary and some fairly dry literature.

The turning point for me came following a trimester when, within our team, we had found significant discrepancies in our marking. Most of this seemed to be related to my marks being lower than those of my colleagues. Numbers on our modules allow for high levels of double-reading and moderation, which had shown up several disagreements. Some of these would have had major implications on students, with pass/fail grades having to be scrutinised. It was around that time, when I really started to understand the importance of constructive alignment (Biggs and Tang, 2011). The work on my patchwork text (an assemblage of formative pieces of writing that were then integrated as a single piece of work) for the Certificate had given me the opportunity to examine in depth how we supported our students in achieving the learning outcomes and how we could perhaps fill some of the gaps more effectively.

Most importantly though, I gained clarity about what I was looking for in students' assignments. My learning helped me recognise that fluent writing style had a significant impact on the way in which I assessed written work. I recognised a tendency to get fed up and annoyed with poor grammar, which sometimes then clouded my view more than a little of the quality of the material underneath. The reflective nature of my studies and learning helped me separate the different aspects of a student's work and to examine it against a range of requirements.

Having felt very disheartened by my poor assessment skills earlier, I was delighted that, as I was progressing through my studies, I was not only becoming clearer in my own mind, but I was able to articulate my assessments much more clearly to my colleagues. My voice was being heard and I was able to hear the voice of others with a listening ear.

As I order my gown for graduation, I am also able to view the effort required for this award in a more balanced way. This was not just about 'ticking a box'. It was very much about ensuring that students receive quality teaching and I have hopefully taken several steps in the right direction on that path. Oh, yes, and that PhD is still to be tackled . . . .

And what is the best way to start a lecture? As with many educational questions we have been unable to provide a single definitive answer. We have seen, though, that it is important to consider such issues as the way in which students learn and the purposes of higher education. A lecture might, of course, not be what is needed at all. But no matter how well you create a case for a different practice there isn't any guarantee that you will adopt the 'better' alternative. When it comes down to it, and a new morning arrives, you might still do nothing more than read out your list of learning outcomes. The choices we make about teaching are determined on more than rational grounds.

REFERENCES

Angelo, T. A., & Cross, K. P. (2005). *Classroom assessment techniques: a handbook for college teachers*. San Francisco: Jossey-Bass.

Ashwin, P., Boud, D., Coate, K., Hallett, F., & Keane, E. (2015). *Reflective teaching in higher education*. London: Bloomsbury.

Biggs, J. B. & Tang, C. (2011). *Teaching for Quality Learning at University: What the Student Does*. Maidenhead: McGraw-Hill Education (UK).

Black, P., Harrison, C., Lee, C., Marshall, B., & Wiliam, D. (2003). *Assessment For Learning: Putting it into Practice*. Maidenhead: Open University Press.

Fink, L. D. (2013). *Creating Significant Learning Experiences: An Integrated Approach to Designing College Courses, Revised and Updated* (Revised and Updated edition). San Francisco: Jossey-Bass.

Freire, P. (2014). *Pedagogy of the Oppressed: 30th Anniversary Edition*. New York: Bloomsbury.

Fry, H., Ketteridge, S., & Marshall, S. (2015). *A Handbook for Teaching and Learning in Higher Education: Enhancing academic practice*. Abingdon: Routledge.

Hussey, T. & Smith, P. (2002). The trouble with learning outcomes. *Active Learning in Higher Education*, 3(3), 220–33.

Hussey, T. & Smith, P. (2003). The uses of learning outcomes. *Teaching in Higher Education*, 8(3), 357–68.

Jaques, D. & Salmon, G. (2007). *Learning in Groups: A Handbook for Face-to-Face and Online Environments*. Abingdon: Routledge.

Jarvis, P. (2012). *Towards a Comprehensive Theory of Human Learning*. London: Routledge.

Laurillard, D. (2013). *Rethinking university teaching: A conversational framework for the effective use of learning technologies*. London: Routledge.

Race, P. (2014). *The lecturer's toolkit: a practical guide to assessment, learning and teaching*. Abingdon: Routledge.

Schunk, D. H. (2012). *Learning Theories: An Educational Perspective* (6th edition). Essex: Pearson.

Yeo, S., Edwards, H., Smith, B. & Webb, G. (2001). Learning from objectives. In *Lecturing: Case Studies, Experience and Practice*. London: Kogan Page.

Chapter 3
The discipline as a locus for enhancement

INTRODUCTION

How did you come to enjoy your subject? Perhaps flashes of insight first hooked you, as concepts and theories came alive. Research allowed you to open up new ideas for yourself. This suggests that a process of discovery is at the heart of any engagement with a subject, and not just the content of a discipline. Disciplines have their own ways of working, habits of thought and characteristic approaches to ideas. They are made up of particular people and given forms of organisation.

When you are teaching, though, it's not just your own mastery of the processes that are inherent to your discipline that matters. Your awareness of these processes and your capacity to introduce them to others are also important. What does it take then to draw students in to the heart of a discipline? How can you learn to do this more effectively? This chapter takes a look at the role that disciplines play in what constitutes excellent teaching, and at the implications for enhancing your teaching. We will need to draw on some further educational theory and social theory to advance the discussion, but hopefully the usefulness of this theory will be apparent.

CONNECTING WITH YOUR SUBJECT

You will be an expert in your discipline, but you may only be a novice when it comes to inducting others into it. One of the first steps in moving forward, then, may be to recognise that there is something of a gap in your own knowledge base for teaching. Bill Hutchings had been teaching for many years to a genuinely good standard, but he describes in Case study 3.1 a particular point in time at which he realised that something was missing in his teaching.

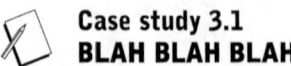

Case study 3.1
BLAH BLAH BLAH

Bill Hutchings, School of Arts, Histories and Cultures, University of Manchester

It was in June that it happened. I had completed what I thought had been a pretty successful teaching year. My second-year undergraduate groups had responded well to their introduction to eighteenth-century literature, a recondite area even to quite advanced students. My third-year groups had contributed fully to the seminars, and had all achieved excellent degrees. Even the poetry of Alexander Pope – our greatest English poet when properly understood, our most boring English poet when not – had seemed to evoke positive responses.

As I basked in the sun of complacency, one of my best third-year students came to thank me for the course, for the materials I had provided and for the helpful teaching. We had a chat about her future plans and her career aims, all of which had been carefully thought through. As we said goodbye until graduation day, she cheerfully added, 'At least now I don't have to read any more poems.' Well, there we were. The sum total of my achievement that year: an excellent student, happy with her degree, kind enough to take the trouble to come and see me (and to leave me a thank you card), now going out into the community with this message for the future of literature: 'at least I don't have to read any more poems'. I toyed with the possibility that she had been displaying characteristically English irony. Had there been a twinkle in her eye as she spoke? But, no; she had been, I was sure, entirely serious.

I looked back at the learning outcomes for my course. There they all were: a detailed knowledge of the works of. . ., deployment of skills of critical and analytical thinking and research at a level appropriate to blah blah . . . skills of written expression blah blah. And, yes, these important outcomes had been achieved, and, yes, my excellent student had well deserved her excellent degree, and I had no reason but to feel satisfied that I had carried out my professional duties. But I went home depressed.

I woke to the realisation that, amidst all the (quality assured) learning outcomes I had so carefully plotted and realised, there were some missing. And these were the very ones that had drawn me to the teaching profession in the first place. The excitement of discovery; the delight in understanding; the intellectual achievement of close and detailed reading; the intensity of discussion and debate; the power of art to open far other worlds and other seas; the chance to communicate all these to sensitive and intelligent people – in sum, the purpose of reading, this was missing.

'The only end of writing is to enable the readers better to enjoy life, or better to endure it', wrote Samuel Johnson in a work that figured largely on the course I had taught. I decided at that point that, whatever else I did, I would try to make my teaching – and the students' learning – consistent with what the authors I was teaching had to say, and with what, ultimately, I felt the subject to be about. And so I looked for learning methods aligned with the basic principles of the subject and...

A lesson that Hutchings learned clearly on that day at the end of an academic year was that the subject itself should colour the way in which it is taught. This is an issue that Rowland (2000) explored, noting as he did that someone teaching design should encourage their students to be inventive in how they learn, while overlap exists between Socratic questioning as both a teaching practice and a philosophical method.

Paying attention to the process of learning goes together with exposing students to the preoccupations of the discipline. When higher education was the preserve of an elite, students might have been expected to discover and master the inner workings of a discipline for themselves. With mass higher education, however, many students arrive poorly prepared for their university studies, and they are likely to find it harder to work out what matters. After all, disciplines have their own characteristic ways of thinking and their own practices, as we shall explore across this chapter. Middendorf and Pace (2004) argued that we have now begun to appreciate more keenly the way that different patterns of thinking characterise the disciplines, and how these patterns affect disciplinary practices. Visualisation, for instance, plays a key role in the sciences, as do practices that enable students to give concrete expression to their mental images on a piece of paper or on a screen. This is a perspective that is also highlighted by social practice theory, an increasingly influential way of looking at professions and disciplines, as well as at teaching itself. Gherardi (2000) argued that knowing and doing are intertwined with each other, as well as by the relationships and the material conditions that accompany them.

The conditions under which one teaches can make a significant difference to what works well. Giving a lecture in a classroom is one thing, but try lecturing amidst the distractions of a laboratory – when the view of the lecturer is obscured for most students! It is not surprising that lecturers in disciplines where teaching occurs in unique environments often share distinctive approaches to their teaching. Shulman (2005) coined the term 'signature pedagogy' to refer to forms of teaching that characteristically apply to given disciplines or professions. A design studio offers quite different possibilities for learning as compared to an operating theatre, say, or to a field.

An excellent teacher is keenly aware of the unique challenges entailed in learning their discipline and supports students in responding to them. Every problem, issue or theory can provide an opportunity explicitly to illustrate something of the internal logic of the discipline: Palmer (2017) calls this teaching from the microcosm. The example in the box below comes from mathematics. This approach enables the tutor to expose the patterns of thought that the students needs to grasp if they are to make sense of the discipline, and its ideas and problems.

Box 3.1
TEACHING FROM THE MICROCOSM

As many readers will know from bitter experience of learning mathematics, if you have failed to understand an initial concept it will be almost impossible to make sense of a more advanced concept that builds on it. For instance, in order to understand how to solve a linear equation, say $2x + 4 = 8$, it helps a great deal to understand the idea of a variable – that is, what the letter x stands for. But students cannot rely on the tutor always identifying the problem for them. They need to able to look at an advanced concept and identify all of the concepts that contribute to it, so that they can then make sure they understand all of these more basic concepts, as one of us explored in a study guide for students (Kahn, 2001).

If the tutor only ever presents the students with an ordered presentation of material, today's typical student is unlikely ever to learn this skill. Effective teaching of mathematics will thus use specific examples to highlight this for students, and provide opportunities for them to develop it.

THE DISCIPLINE AS A LOCUS FOR ENHANCEMENT

 Review point 3.1
ANALYSING YOUR TEACHING

1. Identify some of the basic patterns of thinking that students need to master within your own discipline.

2. How could you induct students into these ways of thinking more directly?

A body of research has grown up around how lecturers conceive their teaching: a (now classic) review identified two broad categories that are outlined in Table 3.1. When adopting an information-focused approach, the tutor primarily seeks to impart knowledge to the student. The tutor's concerns, for instance, may be centred on developing a good set of lecture notes, or on how best to organise the material for the students. By contrast, a focus on the process of learning requires the students to take a more active role. Students are more likely to make their own connections between findings, and thus to experience the discipline as more compelling. This approach is also easier to sustain in the long run, as more depends on the students, and less time needs to be spent preparing materials.

The review by Kember (1997) indicated that tutors who adopt the process-focused approach are significantly more effective in supporting learning than those adopting the information-focused approach. The research, however, also indicates that it is difficult for a lecturer to shift

TABLE 3.1 Conceptions of teaching, after Kember (1997)

Conception of teaching	Description
Information-focused	The tutor believes that it is important to tell the students what they need to know, structuring the information for them.
Process-focused	The tutor sees their role as creating an environment in which the students can learn. This may involve both developing an effective relationship with your students and challenging their preconceptions of your subject.

from one conception to another, and that even when one professes to hold a certain conception of teaching one's actual practice may reflect a different conception, an issue we will explore in Chapter 5 when we consider the difference between espoused theories and theories in action.

We can see the difference between an information-focused approach to teaching one's subject and a process-focused approach that draws its inspiration from what matters in the discipline in the next case study:

Case study 3.2
MAKING CASE STUDY TEACHING REALLY SING

Justin O'Brien, Royal Holloway, University of London

Have you ever asked your class 'What do you think about this week's case study?' and faced a wall of stony silent faces because they had not prepared? I developed an innovative ten-week-long flipped classroom curriculum for my master's level Entrepreneurial Marketing course that did not use PowerPoint projected slides at all. I instead opted to trial an immersive case study approach (sometimes referred to as the Harvard case method). Why did it fail spectacularly? How did a week block teaching experiment in another country as a flying faculty guest professor uncover some insightful critical success factors and restore my passion and confidence for this powerful, experiential pedagogy?

The perfect opportunity, I thought, motivated master's students who were studying entrepreneurship; many of them wanted to develop not only knowledge but also the practical management skills of applying theoretical learnings in a real-world context. As MBA Director this form of experiential learning had proven to be my most popular form of workshop. Students on this particular module were often not engaging with the assigned textbook readings and journal papers, so I invested my whole summer research window to develop my own collection of entrepreneurial short case studies. Surely, I thought, replacing one-way communications with thoughtfully facilitated vibrant conversations would generate multiple light bulb learning moments and motivate students to engage beyond the formal class interactions?

How wrong I was.

After the third week of class, too many students continued to arrive in class unprepared. The cases required a couple of hours' preparation and some reflection to be effective. I ended up providing spontaneous oral summaries

THE DISCIPLINE AS A LOCUS FOR ENHANCEMENT

of the cases (not difficult given I had written them, but still not ideal) and spoon-feeding information to allow my class to respond transactionally to the assigned questions, reducing valuable in-class discussion time. Cases that used real-world YouTube hosted videos as the story telling scaffolding were the most effective (e.g. viral sensations such as the song based United Breaks Guitars and humorous Dollar Shave Club). The case method was an unmitigated disaster in my mind, although student feedback suggested that they did indeed enjoy the learning experiences. Nonetheless, I was profoundly disappointed.

I had noticed that undergraduates in my digital marketing class (part of a 400-strong cohort) were effectively strangers, even though when tasked to interact with each other in small groups they would converse and be on task. Surprisingly, many students were actually very apprehensive about speaking out in class, not wanting to look foolish or saying the wrong thing. I decided to use an invitation to deliver a small-group, 15-hour, week-long, block module as a flying professor in France as a low risk teaching space. I iterated my case study experiment to emphasise process over content, and started by creating powerful teams, investing significant time in the first two afternoons to create a magic circle of trust within the group using a variety of icebreaking, confidence building activities such as speed networking, elevator pitching and Belbin's team role framework. In Management, team working is usually an explicit programme level goal and considered critical for future graduate employability. We worked on technique, understanding not only how to engage with case studies but about the learning outcomes they can and cannot achieve. I gave some hard hitting, frank feedback about their interim performance (2/10) which was an engagement step changer; it seems students are more easily motivated by activities linked to grade outcomes. Activities and concepts were also connected explicitly to value in the working world after graduation and a very powerful focus was provided on the goal, a capstone assessed, plenary case discussion.

Game changing insights?

1. Identifying that, even in small seminars, Management students in the UK and France needed to overcome their inhibitions, find ways to build trust and be explicitly coached to network with peers rather than have their heads in their phones
2. Recognising the need to coach in the process of working with case studies (deep analysis expectations are not obvious to many students)
3. Having the confidence to give frank and open feedback after initial interactions, but before the summative assessment and setting clear stepping stones to success and
4. Finding a low stakes environment to experiment in.

There is still scope, though, for a nuanced understanding of these different conceptions of teaching. Each discipline has its own internal logic, but it is nonetheless the case that all disciplines incorporate concepts within them that open up the possibility of further understanding and inquiry. It is helpful here to distinguish between vertical and horizontal knowledge structures (Bernstein, 2000). Vertical knowledge structures incorporate theories of high generality that integrate apparently disparate phenomena. Such structures are typically associated with the sciences. Fundamental ideas that are at the bottom of a vertical knowledge structure are thus essential to understand thoroughly, such as the idea of a variable in mathematics that we noted above. Such ideas have been referred to as threshold concepts (Meyer and Land, 2006), concepts that when fully understood open up understanding within the discipline and make further progress possible. Horizontal knowledge structures, meanwhile, are characteristically built up through relating distinctive ideas to each other, as occurs in the arts, humanities and social sciences. Concepts in these disciplines that help one make sense of this process of relating ideas to each other are powerful in opening up these disciplines to students. For instance, the social model of disability operates as a threshold concept in social work, helping students to make sense of many different facets of practice in this profession (Morgan, 2012). The research indicates that paying specific attention to threshold concepts in your teaching can pay genuine dividends for student learning, whether this means spending more time on the first encounter of a concept, specifically coming back to explore it in assignments, and so on. Any concern for a process-focused approach needs to contain within it an awareness of the conceptual grounds on which disciplines rest.

DISCIPLINES AS SPACES FOR DIALOGUE

If a discipline is found partly in the processes of discovery that it employs, then it is also the case that it is constituted by specific sets of people. Each discipline incorporates within it a range of academic communities, whether these are departments, long-standing research collaborations, specialist interest groups at conferences, and so on. The nature of these forms of organisation, in terms of membership, aims and identity can be quite different. Some of them even have conflicting and potentially confusing and challenging features; for example, departments are both hierarchical and collegiate, and competitive as well as developmental. Other groupings develop, share and implement development both

THE DISCIPLINE AS A LOCUS FOR ENHANCEMENT

within discrete areas of practice and across institutional and international boundaries. Involvement in them, and identification with them, becomes a logical extension of personal networks. One can think of these various groups as communities of practice.

A community of practice is a collection of people who share a profession or an area of human activity, and who together seek to advance their mutual practices. Roxå and Mårtensson (2009) investigated the conversations that those teaching in universities engage in around their teaching. They found that most staff depend on just a few colleagues for conversations that are private, trusting and intellectually intriguing. A community of practice would only exist around teaching if colleagues are willing to discuss their teaching with each other, and to find new ways forward. Lave and Wenger (1991) were keen to emphasise that newcomers to an existing community of practice need to learn to participate in the community. Part of the shift that is required in becoming an excellent teacher is to see your community of practice in terms of teaching and not simply in terms of research. Working within a community of practice can:

- reduce isolation and the feeling that you are the only person experiencing particular challenges in your teaching
- provide a legitimate voice for an issue or concern about your students
- enable access to 'embedded' or tacit knowledge systems operating within your discipline
- provide a forum in which to act politically (e.g. in advocating change or if critical pedagogy drives your practice)
- send messages to others about your commitment to teaching.

A related notion to that of a community of practice is an institution, a key term from the field of management. When a group of people come together in a family, club, organisation, etc. they characteristically adopt a common set of rules or conventions. A system of norms is referred to in management studies as an institution (Fleetwood, 2008). What typically happens, though, is that these norms promote particular ways of thinking and communicating, and they favour certain decisions over other decisions. In this case it is then said that an institutional 'logic' is in operation. In a traditional academic logic, members of teaching staff focus on the clarity of their explanation or on how to produce slides that can be read by students from the back of a lecture theatre. Of course, the focus has shifted more recently onto student learning, but this is still quite different to a commercial logic in which decisions about teaching are framed above all by considerations of efficiency, and student recruitment or retention. But it might be the case that lecturers in a language department all share certain attitudes to when one should be ready to speak in a target language, or in a science department where it is expected that students will puzzle their way through uncertainty until they have learnt to master what is going on. Staff often expect students to adopt quite quickly the norms of the department within which they are studying. One finds endless complaints from staff when students fail to abide by these norms. Why, though, should students automatically come to share the institutional logic(s) that define life in a given department or disciplinary setting? They haven't given over their working lives to the discipline, and most students only spend a limited amount of time in contact with those who teach them. Students are allowed to set their own priorities – and learning might not always be that high up the list. They are not obliged to value the same things that their lecturers do! Nonetheless, for members of staff it can be hard to see beyond these ingrained norms.

One way to tackle the potential narrowness of life in a department is to include a genuinely wide range of people amongst your colleagues. Towers and Loynes in the case study that follows highlight how the inclusion of a range of other players from within their discipline opened up new ways for students to see their occupation of Outdoor Education, in this case rangers and farmers. And, indeed, new possibilities arose from taking seriously the physical environment within which the students worked. This is quite different from seeing teaching simply as the occasion to be in charge of students. Such different perspectives also become evident when one works with colleagues from other disciplinary settings, an issue that we willl explore in the next chapter.

Case study 3.3
KNOWLEDGE CONSTRUCTION IN OUTDOOR EDUCATION

Danny Towers and Chris Loynes, Department of Science, Natural Resources and Outdoor Studies, University of Cumbria

An opportunity to develop our teaching arose when we were tasked with organising and facilitating a field trip to a remote (in English terms) valley in the

Lake District for an international cohort of masters students studying Outdoor Education. In the UK, the discipline of Outdoor Education entails both process and content ranging across traditional subjects such as physical education and environmental sciences at the same time as foregrounding personal development. The last thing we wanted to be accused of was a neo-colonial teaching of the British 'way' leading to the emergence of a globalised practice in places as far-flung and as different in their landscapes and cultures as Columbia, Kazakhstan and the Philippines. Instead, we sought to problematise the 'occupation' of being an outdoor educator.

Dewey saw 'occupations' in an educational setting as more than just work-related learning, they are epistemological frames for understanding the relationship between the individual experience of the student, the place the learning is situated in and the wider needs of society, such as place-based Outdoor Education. This means that instead of imposing an idea of a profession envisaged by the teachers, the learning is organised through the students taking on a particular occupation in a specific setting (socially and spatially), then developing that particular occupation to follow their interests and the needs of the world (environmental and social).

By educating through occupations and changing to a student-centred approach, we destabilised the established idea of outdoor educator and enabled the students to co-construct a new place-responsive occupation. They explored how to engage with the valley temporally and spatially, inspired by each other, the skills and knowledge of the staff and the valley's material presence. A walk and talk with the ranger began to develop a deeper interpretation of the valley beyond the material encounter. For example, moving through the forest following the trails created by the herd of almost wild cattle and wading upstream in the unconstrained river were powerful experiences brought fully alive by the observations of the ranger who had the perspectives of a longer time and larger purpose. One such critically engaged encounter opened the door for further explorations of the knowledge about the valley held by others, such as a local farmer who explained how his own occupation had been transformed by the changes in the landscape from shepherding to herding wild cattle. We encouraged the students to explore the valley and the opportunities it offered, notice their own talents, interests and motivations and then consider these in the wider context of the needs of society, both broadly and in their own cultural contexts.

We built on the approach of participative inquiry (Reason, 1994) seeking to involve the students as equal participants in their own educational experience. This method fitted well with our intentions for a critical, reflective and democratic pedagogy and the approach was successful in problematizing the occupation of outdoor educator amongst the students, by changing the often taken-for-granted occupation of being a student. Dewey (1938) explained that, when learners perceive that being a student is meaningless and uniformity stifles their exploration they not only struggle to engage with their studies, they may seek other more subversive occupations. Our approach had the effect of critically engaging students in constructing their ideas of the occupation. If the purpose of being a student is learning, the organisation of the educational programme through occupations allowed a more cooperative atmosphere where students as participants developed other ways of imagining what an outdoor educator could or should look like.

If the inclusion of a range of stakeholders can provide a step along the path to excellent teaching, then a community of practice or institution that has built within it a critical dimension is another. In order for collaborative working to have an effective and insightful impact on our teaching we need to adopt a critical stance and to approach it in a way that is objective and analytical. Working with others provides a range of opportunities for critique, analysis and evaluation of our practice that should not be shunned in favour of a 'cosy' relationship that results in little being explored or examined and nothing moving forward. Such collaboration can be created and fostered within a range of critical communities.

Critical communities can take a number of forms, and can involve many different individuals, depending on the purpose of the group. The critical community moves the centre of attention from the individual experience to that of the group, forming a focus for debate, examination of practice, and learning (Campbell, McNamara, and Gilroy, 2004). Examples of critical communities include research groups, working groups, and peer groups within organised programmes of study. The strength of these critical communities lies in the range of knowledge, interest and desire to further understanding and share learning, as a result of critical engagement and discussion through collaborative working, of the group's participants. Critical communities can also be created on a more personal level by individuals seeking to engage with critical debate in order to examine a particular idea, issue or concern within their practice.

DISCIPLINES THAT EVOLVE

What one sees when such criticality is built into your ways of working is teaching that evolves. A critical stance towards your discipline is essential for excellent teaching in the long run. In Case study 3.4 Hulme, Stanyard, Kent and Skipper highlight a way in which their discipline of psychology has been shifting, like so many other disciplines, with a move towards the application of skills and knowledge in everyday life and employment. The interests and drive of students is an important part of what leads a discipline to change.

Case study 3.4
MAKING A DIFFERENCE WITH PSYCHOLOGY

Julie Hulme, Ryan Stanyard, Alexandra Kent and Yvonne Skipper, School of Psychology, Keele University

In 2015, the School of Psychology ran a third year psychology undergraduate option module called 'Social Psychology in the Workplace'. The module was designed by Alexandra Kent, with Yvonne Skipper, to address the university's employability agenda as students formed consultancy firms and used psychology to solve real-world problems. The module was well received by students who took it, but we wanted to increase the number of students who chose the module.

At this time, Julie Hulme joined the module team. She had attended a Higher Education Academy retreat on the future of psychology, and realised that the discipline as a whole was undergoing a shift, which this module reflected. Traditionally, psychology had been taught as an empirical and theoretical science, but there was a growing emphasis on applying psychology to solve problems in everyday life, in employment, and in society. For example, using psychology to change behaviour can improve sustainability, health, and education. Within psychology education, this set of skills and knowledge is known as 'psychological literacy'.

In this context, the team discussed ways to make the module more attractive to students, and we realised that we could broaden the remit of the module, and to address the broader theme of psychological literacy. We consulted with students, changing the title to 'Making a Difference with Psychology', and planned ways to embed problem-solving skills in an engaging way. We needed an innovative approach, and student input was important.

We developed a structure that scaffolds students into independent learning. The module begins with interactive lectures on the psychology of leadership, involving military and police guest speakers. We move to peer learning exercises around the psychology of aspirations, with a speaker from a local charity for looked-after young people, and then into problem-based learning, with students developing ways to improve learning in education and training. Finally, students independently complete a consultancy-style assessment, in which they respond to an 'invitation to tender' (written in consultation with the local organisations, using authentic assessments) proposing a practical intervention and providing an academic rationale. Wherever possible, the students' ideas are fed back to employers and have genuine impact. We all find the idea of the module contributing to the local community exciting!

The module also prepares students for interviews, providing concrete examples of problem-solving skills, and an ability to analyse information critically. This gives students confidence in their abilities, as one student comments:

> Behind every world problem lies human psychology; as students, we discover where theoretical concepts can be applied to issues in society, which is the origin of our initial interest. The module is interactive and allows us to meet the needs of real organisations. Engaging with innovative solutions goes beyond mere academic achievement, preparing us for opportunities where we *can* make a difference.

The module is now popular. Student achievement is strong, and students are proud of their development and problem-solving skills. Partner organisations have also made use of student ideas. As tutors, we find the module immensely rewarding; we see our students become creative thinkers who can draw from their whole psychology curriculum to apply their knowledge, and who enjoy chasing down new information as part of the process.

As a team, we've learned a lot from our experiences. Some of the key lessons include:

- Students enjoy learning challenging material when they can see its relevance to everyday life;
- Employability and everyday problem-solving skills are similar, and students can find this type of learning stimulating;
- Students can be ingeniously creative, and tutors can benefit from this in terms of co-developing mutually rewarding teaching experiences.

If one can find ways to connect with those who are ready critically to take stock of the direction in which a discipline is travelling, then there is significant scope to enhance your own teaching at the same time.

THE DISCIPLINE AS A LOCUS FOR ENHANCEMENT

Change in a discipline, though, need not simply be to do with joining a critical community such as those interested in the future of a discipline such as psychology. Jackson in Case study 3.5 describes the culture of learning that is present within the discipline of fine art, highlighting its signature pedagogy. Fine art as a discipline requires those engaged in it to immerse themselves in its practices. Moreover, Jackson implies that there are no definitive boundaries to either fine art or to fine art education. An expansive approach is required on the part of both staff and students if one is to thrive in this discipline. Expansive learning is the notion that learning can occur in unexpected places, and at times that cannot easily be predicted in advance or in ways that are controlled by teachers (Engeström, 2001). This inevitably means change, as practitioners and students look to stretch the boundaries of the discipline. There is no reason why a signature pedagogy should be static. There is scope for staff to learn from students as part of this expansive approach to the discipline. This is evident scope for expansive learning in relation to the use of digital technology, for instance. The partnership between staff and students, meanwhile, provides the focus for the next chapter.

Case Study 3.5
IN PRAISE OF AN ART SCHOOL EDUCATION OR THE IMPACT OF DRAWING OUT AND LEADING FORTH

Jake Jackson, Glasgow School of Art

It's 3.11p.m. on Saturday 16th June 2018 and, as I sit down to write something of meaning about 'how the nature of fine art as a discipline affects what makes for excellent teaching,' fire continues to ravage inside the very place where my thoughts, experiences, and words on the subject were to emanate from. For me, the source for a response to this proposition was always going to come from my experience as a fine art student and, now, academic member of staff at Glasgow School of Art. Flames have engulfed the Mackintosh Building for the second time in four years.

In light of the ongoing emergency at 167 Renfrew Street, my focus has been drawn to the one thing that remains constant within art school education today. That is, the unique way in which this particular form of education is delivered and negotiated by staff and students alike. The titular phrase 'drawing out and leading forth,' borrowed from Julie Ault and Martin Beck, best describes the philosophy that lies at the heart of what we, as educators, do on a daily basis. The specifics of this approach are determined through what can only be described as an extended and interconnected meaning-making system.

In art school education, this method is established over an extended period of time in order for students to fully immerse themselves in their studies. Students engage in a broad spectrum of experiences, encountering lectures, seminars, one-to-one tutorials, group critique, technical instruction, and critical and theoretical inquiry. Every corner of the art school campus is an accessible site of learning; where full immersion is actively encouraged through the studio, the technical facilities, the lecture theatre, seminar rooms, workshops and the library. Digital technology is endemic, even if differences remain in usage between academic staff and students. It is during this range of learning and teaching activities that the individual students' knowledge and experiences are discussed in order for staff to better understand students' ideas, and their theoretical concerns. By actively listening, staff articulate their practical and theoretical knowledge back to the student in order to help better support their learning.

And yet the location of fine art education is broader still than the school campus. In real terms it is limitless. There are no definitive boundaries. Students are encouraged to seek additional information via their own research and making, enabling them to expand upon their ideas, skills and theoretical concerns. For most art students this expansive understanding takes time to fully comprehend as it sits outside of their previous educational experiences. However, by engaging with this distinctive educational philosophy students gain insights that subsequently become a way of viewing and negotiating the world. Furthermore, what is unique about this form of awareness is that it pertains directly to them, individually; where a range of meanings and interpretations arise, and where infinite possibilities subsequently present themselves.

Within the context of higher education today this specific form of individuated and situated learning is quite unique and is, undeniably, a key component in the process of *becoming* an artist. I will end by saying that I believe this is one of the reason why we have been witness to such emotional outpourings since Friday evening. The depth of feeling expressed by people from around the globe is clear evidence of the powerful nature of the discipline, and those studying or teaching it, and how it continues to have meaning in a world of constant change.

CONCLUSIONS

The disciplinary basis for excellent teaching can be downplayed at times in higher education, as academic development is often led by practitioners who are working across the full range of disciplines and professions that are studied at university. A connection with your discipline, though, offers a profound way to enliven your teaching. And this chapter has been intriguing, we would hope, in suggesting that educational and social theory can usefully open up the relevance of disciplines to teaching! This connection with the discipline can be realised through an awareness of the processes, concepts, practices, networks, communities, and institutions that each discipline incorporates. Teaching enhancement also stems from taking seriously the full range of perspectives and critical voices that are associated with the discipline, as well as the way in which it is changing.

 REFERENCES

Bernstein, B. B. (2000). *Pedagogy, Symbolic Control, and Identity: Theory, Research, Critique*. Lanham, MD: Rowman & Littlefield.

Campbell, A., McNamara, O. & Gilroy, P. (2004). *Practitioner Research and Professional Development in Education*. London: SAGE.

Dewey, J. (1938). *Experience and Education*. New York: Simon and Schuster.

Engeström, Y. (2001). Expansive learning at work: Toward an activity theoretical reconceptualization. *Journal of Education and Work*, *14*(1), 133–56.

Fleetwood, S. (2008). Institutions and social structures. *Journal for the Theory of Social Behaviour*, *38*(3), 241–65.

Gherardi, S. (2000). *Practice-based Theorizing on Learning and Knowing in Organizations*. Thousand Oaks, CA: SAGE.

Kahn, P. E. (2001). *Studying Mathematics and its Applications*. London: Palgrave.

Kember, D. (1997). A reconceptualisation of the research into university academics' conceptions of teaching. *Learning and Instruction*, *7*(3), 255–75.

Lave, J. & Wenger, E. (1991). *Situated Learning: Legitimate Peripheral Participation*. Cambridge: Cambridge University Press.

Meyer, J. H. F. & Land, R. (2006). *Overcoming Barriers to Student Understanding: Threshold Concepts and Troublesome Knowledge*. London: Taylor & Francis.

Middendorf, J. & Pace, D. (2004). Decoding the disciplines: A model for helping students learn disciplinary ways of thinking. *New Directions for Teaching and Learning*, *2004*(98), 1–12.

Morgan, H. (2012). The social model of disability as a threshold concept: Troublesome knowledge and liminal spaces in social work education. *Social Work Education*, *31*(2), 215–26.

Palmer, P. J. (2017). *The Courage to Teach: Exploring the Inner Landscape of a Teacher's Life*. San Francisco, CA: Wiley.

Reason, P. E. (1994). *Participation in Human Inquiry*. Thousand Oaks, CA: SAGE.

Rowland, S. (2000). *The Enquiring University Teacher*. Buckingham: Society for Research into Higher Education & Open University Press.

Roxå, T. & Mårtensson, K. (2009). Significant conversations and significant networks–exploring the backstage of the teaching arena. *Studies in Higher Education*, *34*(5), 547–59.

Shulman, L. S. (2005). Signature pedagogies in the professions. *Daedalus*, *134*(3), 52–9.

Chapter 4

A partnership with students in learning and teaching

INTRODUCTION

Do you think you have a good working relationship with your students? Are they enthusiastic, responsive and enquiring learners: essentially, are they engaged? If the answer is yes to all of those questions, then well done! But do you consider them your partners in learning? Working in partnership with students is a hot topic. Any online search in this area brings up a range of academic papers and information on this subject from institutional, student and sector perspectives, and a whole raft of publications from bodies such as the National Union of Students and Advance HE. But what do we mean when we talk about 'working in partnership'? It has to begin at one level with student engagement, as without this there could not be any kind of partnership working. But what do we mean by this phrase? Philippa Levy, in Healey, Flint and Harrington (2014, foreword) notes that: '"Student engagement" has become a core aim for the sector and, increasingly, is being linked to ideas about students' roles as partners in their higher education communities.'

Student engagement as a sector-wide aim reflects a broad spectrum of activity including national student surveys and institutional student partnership agreements, through to engagement at the cohort and individual level where teaching and learning related activities are potentially co-constructed by lecturers and students together. 'Engagement' is in itself a contested term (Carey, 2013; Buckley, 2018) and, as Kahn (2017: 61) notes, we need to distinguish between 'students undertaking a partnership with their educators' and other forms of engagement such as 'giving a response to a consultation . . . or by [students] taking a lead of their own' in order to be clear in what we mean by engaging with our students in partnership working.

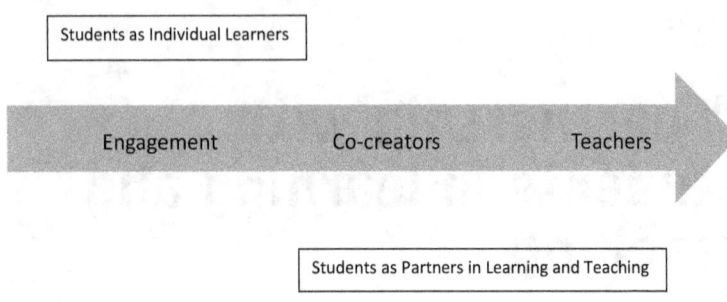

FIGURE 4.1 Student partnership journey in learning and teaching

For Healey et al. (2014: 7): 'partnership represents a sophisticated and effective approach to student engagement because it offers the potential for a more authentic engagement with the nature of learning itself and the possibility for genuinely transformative learning experiences'. In this chapter we're going to look at two specific areas of potential partnership working that have the potential to develop such 'genuinely transformative learning experiences' and to help you to think about how these approaches might support you in developing your teaching: students as co-creators of curricula and students as teachers. This will be situated within a discussion around student learning in order to reflect on how you can support your students in a 'more authentic engagement with the nature of learning itself', contextualised within your own area of practice.

New spaces for practice and potentially new different educational paradigms need to be created in order to support us in moving into this territory. Working in partnership in this way with our students is not something that can be entered into as easily as developing a new seminar structure or introducing a blog into an online course. In supporting you in identifying these spaces for teaching development we'll also consider the opportunities presented and the challenges raised if you are to employ a successful partnership working approach to developing your teaching.

STUDENTS AS CO-CREATORS

In order to get maximum benefit out of the idea of working in a teaching and learning partnership with students, we need to think again about the traditional roles and identities of 'teachers' and 'learners'. We also need to reflect on the changing nature of higher education, often instigated by developments in digital technologies and demands from a technologically driven workplace – something we'll look at in greater detail in Chapter 7. Life-long learning is now an idea that has very much become a reality as our graduates can expect to have portfolio careers rather than one job for life, with the associated demands of regular up-skilling or re-training. Part of this change is also the expectation that students will play a more active role in their learning journey through higher education. What might this look like? For some students, it may be engaging more proactively with their courses as class representatives or making the decision to sign up for a work placement or internship; that is, responding to the available opportunities. This kind of engagement can create mutually beneficial partnership working for everyone involved. In the following case study Bethan Wood and Sophie N. Brett (student) from the School of Interdisciplinary Studies at the University of Glasgow (Dumfries), discuss what they took away from an example of partnership working with an external organisation, whose views are also included.

Case study 4.1
LEVERAGING STUDENT CAPITAL

Bethan Wood and Sophie N Brett, University of Glasgow (Dumfries)

Our campus is set in a rural location with access to the local living laboratory and within easy travelling distance of a number of environmental organisations. It is the ideal location for an environmental degree programme.

Bethan – My BSc programme includes an optional 60 credit placement course in the third year. This approach had worked well on an MSc programme I created and I was keen for the undergraduates to have the same opportunity – regardless of ability. Some of the local organisations already contributed to some of the courses through specialist talks, lectures, field visits and classes. It was therefore an easy step to raise the prospect of placements. As a result, about 80 per cent of students select a placement and locally 13 organisations have so far facilitated student placements, with some now offered on a yearly basis.

We have found that:
- Our students gain skills, and experience the reality of a work environment. This can lead to a lot of personal as well as professional learning which can mean that sometimes they find it is not the one for them.

- They can link the University's graduate attributes to their personal learning goals and can then articulate these skills on their CVs, enhancing their employability.
- The employers frequently see the students as future employees. This has then led to further partnerships with the student: honours projects, part-time work, research, and higher degrees.
- I have also benefited and learned new things from: specialist talks on courses, field classes, joint supervision of research students, and publishing papers together.

Sophie – Keen to ensure employability beyond undergraduate studies, choosing a credit-bearing work placement in collaboration with a local organisation over a taught course was a decision I easily made. Not only was it a great opportunity for me to gain experience of a 'real-world' work place, it also facilitated networking with professionals in an area of interest – potentially for future career progression or study.

- The accompanying assessments enhanced my experience by encouraging 'real-world' thinking, rather than the traditional formats you would expect from a taught course.
- Critically evaluating and reflecting on oneself and progress in relation to a real position with real consequences beyond the bubble of University, and being able to articulate this was a valuable experience I continue to benefit from.

Our campus is relatively small in a rural setting, and so having skills to build and maintain relationships outside academia are an important part of forging a career in the local area. While my journey brought me back to academia, the impact of my research relies on establishing and sustaining strong partnerships with local communities and organisations in rural areas. Thus, my work placement has proved invaluable to me.

Employers also valued the contribution the students make to their organisation.

- The students were a real asset to the organisation and coped well with the demanding and varied workload – the willingness to 'try anything they were asked to do' was particularly appreciated.
- The student could undertake the work/projects that we wanted to do, but which our own staff simply had not had the time to do.
- Networking with the university/staff and the benefits of the experience meant that other departments within my organisation are now looking for placement students!

The three partners have benefited from this enhanced engagement. Placements could be included in any taught degree programme; whether as an option instead of a dissertation, or as an alternative to the equivalent credits in taught courses, and provide an authentic, practical and engaging route into multi-partnership working.

For other students, however, this kind of active learning can be more about creating new opportunities by assuming a direct involvement in the learning and teaching process through co-constructing that experience with their teachers. Viewing students as co-constructors of their own learning and teaching opportunities moves us away from the idea of students as simply passive consumers of educational didacticism. It brings to life the theory which extols active learning as the key to successful learning – but it may also be seen as taking it way beyond that idea and into a realm where students may know little about what they are trying to achieve, or can be argued as not 'belonging' to them. Some students will be drawn to this idea and others turned off by it. Some will be genuinely engaged by the process as a pedagogic device while others may take the view that it is 'our job', and not that of the students, to get involved in designing their learning experiences; parents or other funders may take a similar view. Positions on this topic will be adopted in relation to the individual's conception of what university study 'is' – what it should look like, the roles that people should play within it, and what the outcomes should be. For those who associate 'good teaching' with increased contact hours, regardless of the role that the students take in this process, partnership working may not be an attractive option; nor may it make much sense to them. We are the teachers, who do the teaching, while the students are those who do the learning. Isn't that the way it's supposed to work?

From our perspective as teachers, however, to what extent can a partnership approach be seen as an extension of the student-centred model of teaching and learning? From a 'sage on the stage' didactic model to 'guide on the side' facilitation model; and now to 'partner *at* the side' co-construction model? For some of us, an initial reaction may be that students are not in a position to make these decisions in an informed and meaningful way. Bovill and Bulley (2011: 8) make a useful comment which addresses this concern:

> in relation to other academic knowledge and skills we often support students to develop their capabilities, for example, with academic writing and presentation skills. Therefore, if a particular level of ASP [active student participation] in curriculum design is considered desirable and beneficial, equivalent support and guidance for students (and staff) may be necessary.

The idea of student co-construction of the curriculum as part of the overall learning process rather than an exceptional extra, contributing to the development of graduates' attributes and value-added skills development within potentially every course of study, may suddenly make the idea appear much more attractive. It can also help to encourage an attitudinal shift – for both ourselves and our colleagues – in order to help create a new space for the development of working with our students in this way.

However, let's not get ahead of ourselves but rather start with what we know and with which we are familiar. Is working *with* students, the same as partnership working? Is obtaining feedback from students just 'good practice', while acting on it reflects partnership working and the first steps towards working together on curriculum re-development? It may be that this is co-construction of the curriculum by the back door and that we may be engaged in a range of activities that do comprise partnership working without actually realising it. Good – and by 'good' we mean honest and thoughtful – student feedback has the potential to significantly enrich and enhance our practice. Learning from student feedback can help to develop your teaching in a number of ways including:

- leading you to a better understanding of how students learn;
- appreciating what works and what doesn't in terms of your teaching practice;
- 'road testing' new teaching approaches;
- responding effectively to student concerns or anxieties;
- and validating your current approach to practice.

Students can also benefit from the shared learning experience that can be created by effectively designed feedback methods. In the following case study from the Arts Institute at Bournemouth, Val Fisher shares her experience of how feedback from students on her art and design course illuminated the value-added learning that had developed from their studies, including student understanding of pedagogy.

Case study 4.2
ADDING VALUE THROUGH STUDENT LEARNING ABOUT TEACHING

Val Fisher, Arts Institute at Bournemouth

Lecturers are increasingly being faced with a dilemma. Where it was once possible to conduct small group sessions and create the ideal learning environment, increasing student numbers and larger groups now present challenges to those traditional models. Faced with one such large class, working in a practice-based art and design subject, I aimed to avoid the passive learning that can take place in lectures through the development of a 'show and tell' sketchbook of development work. However, the challenge was in recreating the learning dynamic of small group teaching, usually facilitated by a 'flick-through' of the sketchbook, in a lecture class of 40 students. I addressed this issue by photographing the pages to illustrate the development process and showed this as a PowerPoint presentation. Prior to this the students undertook a critique of my designs, and then, unaware of the context of my work, presented their analysis to the group. At the appropriate point in the lecture I talked them through the designs they had previously analysed. They were pleased to discover that their powers of analysis and deduction were astute, and I was pleased that their feedback indicated that my designs were successful. I did take away some ideas for improvements though.

The written feedback from students at the end of the lecture was very positive but also significant in that it worked on several levels. I was most interested by the comments about the session from the point of view of lesson planning and particularly the student understanding of pedagogy. The comments indicated that the students had evaluated the session not purely as a learning experience for themselves, but from a teaching and learning perspective – how to use visual aids, how to structure a two and a half hour session, how to vary the pace through the use of different methods, how to get the group to interact. They then went on to use what they had learned in the peer assisted learning scheme where third year students work with first years. It was a 'red letter' day for me, showing how verbal and written feedback were instrumental in informing student learning about their subject, my own learning about my practice as a designer, my practice as a teacher, and student learning about teaching practice!

The driver here to create a new space for this kind of development was turning a potentially passive learning environment into one that facilitated student engagement and active learning. But the emergent learning that came out of this was the extent to which her students engaged not just with the activity itself but in how they adopted a meta-analytic approach to the whole experience, demonstrating a 'student understanding of pedagogy'. How might this level of student engagement be harnessed in other ways?

In the following case study, Sue Beckingham explains how she approached her students in Business Information Systems and Technology at Sheffield Hallam University to look at co-construction of the curriculum. The opportunity to create a new space for development was provided in this case by social media. Three different stages of the partnership approach are discussed: co-creation of resources, ensuring the sustainability of the approach, and the value-added provided for the student experience.

Case study 4.3
SMASH: SOCIAL MEDIA FOR ACADEMIC STUDIES AT HALLAM

Sue Beckingham, Sheffield Hallam University

I became increasingly curious how social media, so easily accessible via a mobile phone, was being used to communicate and collaborate in the context of the student learning experience. Reflecting on my own use for informal learning and CPD, I wanted to know whether students also utilised social media beyond *social interactions*, and how this might be enhancing student engagement. There was only one way to find out and that was to ask my students.

I initially approached four students who'd attended the Social Media for Learning in Higher Education Conference at Sheffield Hallam University. Following the event I asked if they would like to form a special interest group to explore this topic further. This led to the creation of a student-led group named SMASH: Social Media for Academic Studies at Hallam. I adopted the role of mentor and we met fortnightly face-to-face and communicated online using social media.

Through our partnership, a framework was created which considers three strands of social media use for learning:

1. Learning Activities: supporting staff in identifying and using social media tools for communication and collaboration within and beyond the classroom.
2. Organising Learning: supporting students and staff to identify and use relevant social media tools to curate and organise information relating to learning.
3. Showcasing Learning: supporting students in preparing digital portfolios to openly share outcomes and projects to develop a professional online presence.

This approach was used to develop a collection of useful resources that would stimulate discussion around the use of social media; and these were shared with other tutors and students on our course. The result was that not only did we develop ways to enhance my teaching, so did my peers. Rich discussions transpired leading to new ideas that will be implemented across the course that students and staff value.

Initially I thought the project might fizzle out at the end of the academic year as one member graduated and two went on placement. However the remaining student was keen to take the project forward and reached out to her peers. Three new students joined the group, plus one of the students out on placement chose to continue to be involved remotely through social media. She will take up the lead in the new academic year and is already recruiting peers to join her.

From my perspective I will continue to explore student partnerships to enhance approaches in my own practice and hope to inspire others to do so too. I feel that the key aspects to the continued success of the SMASH project include:

- giving students ownership
- helping them develop confidence to put forward their perspectives
- ensuring that the students involved each recognise the skills they're developing and how this valuable evidence can be added to their CVs
- celebrating their achievements using social media – this was valued immensely.

With thanks to the students involved in this student partnership to date: Sher Khan, Ola Mazur, Jess Paddon, Callum Rooney, Matty Trueman, Abby Wood and Corran Wood.

These two case studies identify different points on a spectrum of student partnership working through a co-construction approach. They have also highlighted two examples of what enabled it to happen: a drive to change the nature of the learning environment and the use of social media. Both of these drivers were highly relevant to both staff and students and allowed for positive engagement and follow-through. We will all have our own comfort level – staff, students and institutions – with the extent to which we might embrace or adopt such an approach. Bovill and Bulley (2011: 5) outline a 'ladder of student participation in curriculum design', which represents a continuum of levels of potential student participation

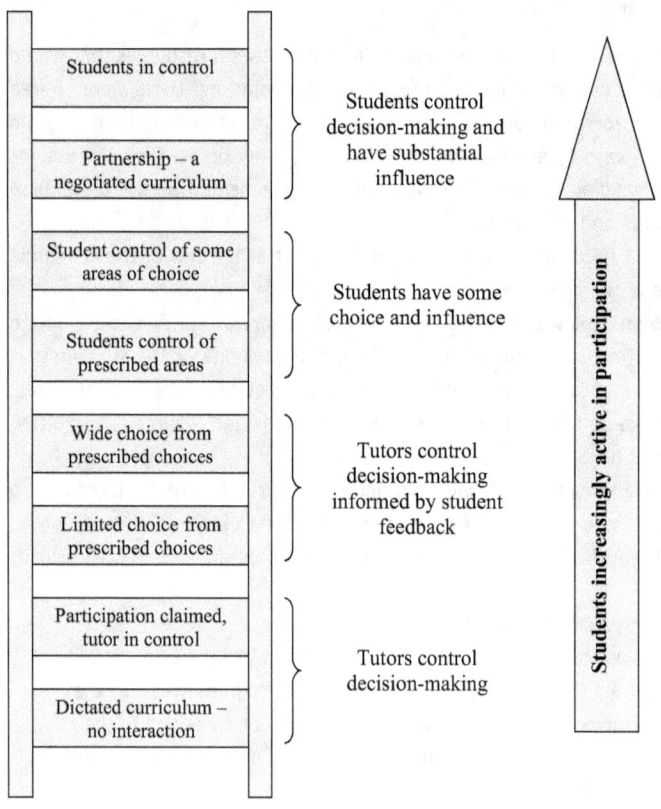

FIGURE 4.2 Ladder of student participation in curriculum design (Bovill and Bulley, 2011)

ranging from a tutor-controlled dictated curriculum with no student interaction through eight steps or stages, up to students being in control of decision-making and having substantial influence. In practical terms, Bovill and Bulley identify these steps as the lowest rung on the ladder beginning with students simply turning up for class, going all the way through to the topmost rung where students are developing their own learning outcomes and designing projects (2011: 7).

There are obviously several steps in between these two extremes and part of examining the idea of working with students in this way is to explore your levels of comfort with this process. Co-construction can be perceived by some to be a risky as well as an innovative undertaking. It raises a lot of questions for you, your students – and for your institution. It can also provide excellent opportunities for peer learning and support in addition to individual student learning, as we see in the following case study, which outlines the experiences of staff and students working together on the Student Active Engagement in Learning (SAEL) project at Royal Holloway, University of London. The case study was developed by Becky Thomas along with her students Anju Kirby and Billy Dyall, and provides an insight into the aims and outcomes of the project; the thoughts from all three on the experience from their individual perspectives; and additionally, as with Case study 4.3, an example of partnership working in the development of the case study itself.

Case study 4.4
STUDENT ACTIVE ENGAGEMENT IN LEARNING – THE SAEL PROJECT

<small>Becky Thomas, Anju Kirby and Billy Dyall, Royal Holloway, University of London</small>

Higher education policy is continually emphasising the importance of students' active engagement in their learning and the benefits that can be gained by students playing an active role in shaping this learning, so we approached this project with the view that our students would be active partners. Funding from the School of Biological Sciences allowed us to employ two students for four weeks, full time, on the SAEL project (Students Active Engagement in Learning). They were given the brief that we wanted to develop a series of stimulating and varied teaching materials to assist our students in their development. In response, the students created their own questionnaire, reviewed the data and decided on two areas to target: students' transition to university and employability, which resulted in the following project outputs.

- To support effective student transition, the students created a 'survival pack' sent out to students a month before they arrived at university.
- The survival pack contained videos and screencasts covering information about daily life and how to make the most of lectures and labs, creating an excellent introduction for new students.
- To support employability they created a further set of resources including a series of videos from our alumni talking about their career paths after graduation, helping students identify potential careers and providing tips on how to get there.

Billy – I jumped at the opportunity to take on an integral role within the department with student experience in mind. Using our own experience and that of my peers we have created a range of engaging resources which have successfully welcomed and supported new members of the student community.

Becky – From a staff perspective, the benefits of this project have been threefold: to the students on our programmes who benefit from the resources created, to the staff who get to work with dynamic students and to the students working on the project.

Anju – I have thoroughly enjoyed being a part of the SAEL project. It has allowed me to have an active, creative role and feel involved within my department, whilst developing mixed-media resources for new students which I would have greatly appreciated when I joined the university.

Becky – Students are often consulted about their learning (e.g. course feedback forms), but it is much less common to see partnerships between staff and students where students are really brought to the heart of the teaching and learning process; they may not yet be 'discipline or pedagogic experts' but they have a much clearer knowledge of what it means to be a student in today's higher education environment. Partnerships with students are a fantastic opportunity to work with individuals with a genuine understanding of the challenges faced by learners in higher education, and with support and guidance this can result in the creation of resources that are of real benefit.

This example of partnership working approached the idea of co-construction by framing it within a specific project. Adopting this method can provide a good testing ground for the concept in advance of potentially mainstreaming it within the broader curriculum. The focus of the project was also on a topic that the individual students had experience of personally and was both relevant and meaningful to them. Providing this kind of hook into a model of co-construction is vital to a successful outcome. The level of student knowledge of the material also provided additional validity and authenticity to the co-construction approach.

Review point 4.1
IDEAS INTO PRACTICE

Having now heard from several colleagues about how a model of co-construction has worked for them, reflect on these questions to help you think about how partnership working through co-construction might work in your practice.

- To what extent would this involve a culture change at your university?
- How receptive might your students be to the idea – or not?
- What vehicles currently exist that might help to mobilise these ideas?
- Can you create new vehicles?
- What are the potential barriers – or risks?
- What might be the benefits?
- How might working with students in this way help you to develop your teaching?
- And as a result, positively impact your students' learning?

STUDENTS AS TEACHERS

Student partnerships in teaching and learning can extend beyond models of co-construction into the idea of students as teachers. We are already familiar with the idea of postgraduate students taking on teaching or demonstrating roles but identifying undergraduates with this role is much less common. So why would we want to do this?

- Teaching is one of the best ways of learning.
- It will support student engagement in active learning.

- Students often learn best from one another, through peer learning.
- The act of teaching develops communication and presentation skills.

As we found earlier in this chapter when we looked at student feedback, we can often be working on the fringes of student partnership activity without actually realising or acknowledging it – or giving the students credit for it. Students will already be engaging in collaborative activities that support learning in a number of ways, such as:

- answering one another's questions posted on discussion boards or social media platforms
- undertaking peer assessment
- providing feedback on peer presentations
- collaborative learning online
- leading debates, discussions or seminars
- structured activities, such as authoring Wikipedia pages or personal blogs related to their area of study.

Healey et al. (2014: 8) note that '[e]ngaging students as teachers and assessors in the learning process is a particularly effective form of partnership' and we can see an example of this in action in our next case study. Neil Hudson tells us about the approach to champion students as teachers developed at the Royal (Dick) School of Veterinary Studies, University of Edinburgh.

Case study 4.5
AND JUNO CAME TOO

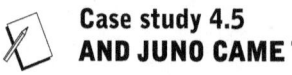

Neil Hudson, Royal (Dick) School of Veterinary Studies, University of Edinburgh

At our university we have introduced a novel Undergraduate Certificate in Veterinary Medical Education. A key responsibility of veterinary professionals is the education of clients, colleagues and students undertaking placements. So, we wanted to formally recognise the important role that students play in the School's teaching and learning processes and foster students as partners in education through the development of this Certificate. We surveyed students and future veterinary employers to see what they thought of such an idea. The reaction was really positive and the comments helped us in the design of our programme. So, in 2014 we took the leap and started this optional programme which the clinical students can take in parallel to their main degree.

The programme is modular and students can enrol in their third year. There are core and elective components, incorporated into a reflective portfolio, with completion over the final three years of the veterinary degree. Our first cohort of 22 completed their Certificate in summer 2017 and we currently have a total of 120 enrolled with us. A small subset can take their training a step further under our staff mentorship by embarking on applying for Associate Fellowship of the Higher Education Academy (AFHEA). Six students have achieved this to date, with several other applications underway. This is very exciting for us as our first successful AFHEA student was the first veterinary student in the UK to achieve this qualification.

One educational strand implemented in the Certificate is the opportunity for our veterinary students to become involved in outreach workshops and school visits to foster the link with young people aspiring to enter higher education. As an illustration of how this has grown, in the first year of running the programme, 26 of our students have been involved in a total of 10 outreach educational activities, with exposure to over 900 school pupils. The number of activities has increased and the reach is not just within Edinburgh and surrounds, but some of our students have done similar activities in their previous schools, including further afield in Scotland, England and even Hong Kong and Alaska!

The work with schools has really been embraced by our students and it has been great forging partnerships in this area. For me personally, this has been incredibly humbling and rewarding. Seeing our students in action with school pupils, inspiring them and reaching out with their developing skill set, has been fantastic. I have also learnt so much in terms of my own teaching, learning from my students and from the school teachers, for whom I have the highest admiration. It has broken down perceived barriers between staff and students and now we are very happy to share tips and learn from each other; the Certificate has really provided the backdrop to allow this. It has been a real two-way process and that is what partnerships are all about. Plus my dog, Juno, who accompanies us on many of these teaching activities, has really enjoyed herself, being the centre of attention as we teach pupils how to care for their pets.

Our students have also developed and been involved in activities as part of their Certificate that include helping fellow students with peer-assisted learning activities and charitable work such as tutoring refugees and helping homeless people with their pets. Through this programme our students have been fantastic ambassadors and inspirational role models. Truly, they are our partners in education.

Neil Hudson's work in this area has created a distinctive space for development of a partnership working approach, to which his students have risen admirably. Their willingness to be stretched and challenged has seen them certify their learning as teachers and also take ownership of the idea, with increasing numbers engaging with the opportunity to take their learning a step further in becoming Associate Fellows of the HEA – accredited by Advance HE. In supporting his students to become teachers, Neil is also supporting them in developing their professionalism. Can you see similar opportunities within your context for your students?

OPPORTUNITIES AND CHALLENGES

What is it that you might be trying to achieve if you adopt a partnership working approach with your students? What benefits might there be for your students in terms of more meaningful, relevant and authentic learning; greater inclusivity; or greater understanding of how assessment supports learning? A partnership implies benefits to both sides so to what extent might working with students in this way help *you* to develop your teaching? Indeed, there is the possibility that:

> student involvement in course design could lead to much more radical change in higher education: ending what is perceived by some to be the domination of curricula by Western, white and male thinking, and opening them up to be more representative of university communities that are increasingly diverse, and ever more internationalised.
>
> (Havergal, 2015)

We saw from the case studies above that we need a reason or an opportunity – a driver – to implement this kind of approach and for it to work effectively. What might that look like in your practice? Do any of these statements resonate with you and might they provide that driver?

- My course is no longer 'working'
- My students are not engaged
- I want to make my classroom environment more participatory
- There is funding available to develop a student-centred project
- The student voice needs to come through more clearly in my practice

(adapted from Bovill, 2014)

PARTNERSHIP IN LEARNING AND TEACHING

TABLE 4.1 A planned approach to partnership working

What's the driver, reason, or opportunity?
What can you do to make it happen?
What will be involved?
How will this develop effective partnership working with your students?
What might the students get out of it?
What might you get out of it?

If you have an idea in mind, try using the planning approach outlined in Table 4.1 to scope the project and then to reflect on what the possible outcomes could be.

In this case study Richard Sober and Anne Llewellyn talk us through their development of a co-creation and authentic learning approach with their students on the Interior Architecture and Interior Design courses at Teesside University. Using the planning approach outlined above, they reflect on the opportunity to develop a partnership approach, the action taken, and the ways in which their students benefited from this approach.

Case study 4.6
A PLANNED APPROACH

Richard Sober and Anne Llewellyn, Teesside University

What was the teaching opportunity?

Part of the top floor of our University Library was designated as a postgraduate learning space and whilst the lower four floors had undergone major refurbishment, this floor remained unchanged since an earlier refit. The space consisted of a silent student area and a more social learning space. However, in practice both areas were treated as individual study rooms. The design students were asked to redesign it to more clearly represent the spatial definition from the perspective of being learners themselves, to increase social interaction and use of and engagement with the spaces. This presented an opportunity for collaborative working between our students and the University Library.

What did you do?

The students worked collaboratively in small practice teams to produce the designs for the postgraduate study rooms. This approach replicates industrial practice as well as developing team and leadership skills. The key tasks involved surveying the space, analysing user requirements, developing the brief from the client's initial aims and requirements and ultimately producing design solutions.

What was involved?

The project was undertaken over a 12-week period and culminated in a presentation to the client in the form of a professional pitch rather than an academic presentation. Throughout the process the students were supported by design tutors and had access to advice from the Library team but were encouraged to lead their own projects and apply their own expertise and perspective of defining spaces for distinct learning types. Students received feedback on both their design and presentation skills.

How did this approach develop partnership working with your students?

This authentic practice and problem-based learning followed the principle of students as producers defined by Neary (2010) as 'a fundamental principle of curriculum design whereby students learn primarily by engagement in real research projects, or projects which replicate the process of research in their discipline. Engagement is created through active collaboration amongst and between students and academics.' This demonstrates the impact of this approach in terms of product, process and personal dimensions of knowledge gain and when examining the process it fulfils many of the latest aims for innovative and student centred pedagogy.

What did the students get out of it?

The benefits for the students involved were working on a real-life project with a real client and real users. This creative project connected teaching and research with students at the centre of the activity and the problem-based learning approach allowed students to apply critical thinking and analytical skills to a tangible disciplinary problem coupled with their research skills. Through the project, students developed both key discipline and more general employability skills such as team working, problem solving and professional presentation skills but with the added authenticity of applying their skills and knowledge to a real problem, the solution to which had a real chance of being taken forward.

What did you get out of it?

The student as producer approach links authentic learning with research in-formed teaching. This takes the lecturer and learner relationship much further towards facilitation and a module's learning outcomes beyond being created simply for assessment purposes.

CONCLUSIONS

The case studies in this chapter have shown students: taking advantage of curriculum opportunities which allowed for the development of meaningful learning partnerships for everyone involved; adopting a more proactive lead in curriculum development with their teachers, benefiting themselves and their peers; and enhancing their professional skills through assuming roles as teachers themselves. In developing your teaching through partnership working with students, there are a number of aspects you need to think about.

- What are the anticipated benefits or opportunities for all involved?
- Why might your students choose to get involved? Are these benefits obvious?
- How will the overall power balance in the relationship be managed? And who will do the managing?
- What are the contingency plans if the relationship fails to work as anticipated? Would this simply be a lost opportunity or does a central aspect of your approach to learning and teaching hinge on the success of a partnership working approach?

Having a clear conception of what partnership working might look like in your context is an important starting point. This can vary in relation to discipline (Crawford, Horsley, Hagyard and Derricott, 2015: 15), experience in this area, and the ultimate objective and intended outcomes for the partnership. Keeping the HEA's 'values in partnership' (ibid.: 2015: 17) in mind when you're thinking about where to start may be a good place to begin.

Developing partnership working approaches with our students, either through co-construction of the curriculum or encouraging our students to take on more of a teaching role, will inspire some but terrify others. It might also invoke hostility and confusion, where colleagues feel

TABLE 4.2 HEA framework for student engagement through partnerships (after Crawford et al., 2015)

Authenticity – the rationale for all parties to invest in partnership is meaningful and credible.	Honesty – all parties are honest about what they can contribute to partnership and about where the boundaries of partnership lie.	Inclusivity – there is equality of opportunity and any barriers (structural or cultural) that prevent engagement are challenged.
Reciprocity – all parties have an interest in, and stand to benefit from working and/or learning in partnership.	Trust – all parties take time to get to know one another and can be confident they will be treated with respect and fairness.	Courage – all parties are encouraged to critique and challenge practices, structures and approaches that undermine partnership, and are enabled to take risks to develop new ways of working and learning.
Plurality – all parties recognise and value the unique talents, perspectives and experiences that individuals contribute to partnership.	Responsibility – all parties share collective responsibility for the aims of the partnership, and individual responsibility for the contribution they make.	Empowerment – power is distributed appropriately and ways of working and learning promote healthy power dynamics.

threatened by these developments. Yet, while there are undoubtedly challenges and potential risks associated with embracing this approach, we should not be closed off to considering how it might potentially enhance our teaching and ultimately our students' learning. Indeed, if we are to continue to act as 'gatekeepers to the curriculum' (Bovill and Bulley, 2011: 8) what restrictions are we placing on the insights that might be gained from engaging in a partnership approach with our students?

 REFERENCES

Bovill, C. & Bulley, C. J. (2011). A model of active student participation in curriculum design: exploring desirability and possibility. In C. Rust (ed.) *Improving Student Learning (ISL) 18: Global Theories and Local Practices: Institu-*

tional, Disciplinary and Cultural Variations. Oxford: Oxford Brookes University; Oxford Centre for Staff and Learning Development. University of Glasgow eprint. http://eprints.gla.ac.uk/57709/ [Online, accessed 16 September 2018].

Bovill, C. (2014). Co-creation of learning and teaching: background, evidence and strategies for success. Presentation to the University of Edinburgh PTAS Forum. 10 June 2014.

Buckley, A. (2018). The ideology of student engagement research. *Teaching in Higher Education*, 23(6), 718 – 32.

Carey, P. (2013). Student as co-producer in a marketised higher education system: A case study of students' experience of participation in curriculum design. *Innovations in Education and Teaching International*, 50(3), 250 – 60.

Crawford, K., Horsley, R., Hagyard, A. & Derricott, D. (2015). *Pedagogies of Partnership: What works*. York: The Higher Education Academy.

Havergal, C. (2015). 'Should students be partners in curriculum design?' *Times Higher Education Supplement*.

Healey, M., Flint, A. & Harrington, K. (2014). *Engagement through Partnership: Students as Partners in Learning and Teaching in Higher Education*. York: The Higher Education Academy.

Kahn, P. E. (2017). Higher education policy on student engagement: Thinking outside the box. *Higher Education Policy*, 30(1), 53 – 68.

Neary, M. (2010). *Student as producer: A pedagogy for the avant-garde? Learning Exchange*, 1(1). Lincoln University. http://eprints.lincoln.ac.uk/4186/ [Online, accessed 16 September 2018].

Chapter 5

Engaging with reflective practice

INTRODUCTION

The concept of reflective practice is one with which you will be familiar if you have engaged with a Postgraduate Certificate in teaching and learning, or from reading around the teaching in higher education literature, or perhaps from discussing with colleagues. Some areas of practice, such as nursing and midwifery, also have a strong tradition of reflection as a way of thinking and practising within the discipline; other discipline areas place less overt emphasis on reflection but it will implicitly inform the ways in which practice is developed and enhanced. You may also be aware of the associated concept of reflexivity, which we'll look at in greater detail in Chapter 7, where we consider drivers within our practice.

This chapter will look at the ways in which we can understand the role of reflection within our own context and how we can integrate a reflective approach within our day-to-day activity – without it feeling like just one other thing that has to be done. We'll consider a range of approaches that you might want to try, both for yourself and with your students, and the case studies will look at how some of these approaches have worked in practice; and as a result, what might work for you in developing your teaching.

IDENTIFYING REFLECTIVE PRACTICE

Evaluating your practice is key to developing your teaching. Whatever its focus, evaluation involves taking a step back and thinking about the kind of teacher you are currently, the kind of teacher you would like to be, and the ways in which you would like your teaching to develop. Evaluating our current practice can tell us about where we are now, but more

ENGAGING WITH REFLECTIVE PRACTICE

importantly it can support us in moving towards being the kind of teacher that we would like to be in the future. To achieve this we need to do more than just look at our practice as related to us via a student evaluation form and then file it for posterity. We need to actively engage with the information in some way. One of the ways you can set about this process is by developing and cultivating a more *reflective* approach.

How can you adopt a reflective approach in your practice? The terms 'reflective practice', 'reflective practitioner' and 'reflexivity' are common currency in text books on teaching and learning and courses on academic practice. But to what extent has the discussion penetrated our consciousness, and the ways in which we teach and support learning? Admittedly, the language of reflective practice can be off-putting. Writings on the subject are various, in both length and quality, and it can prove an elusive concept to grasp where words can only too easily serve to obfuscate rather than clarify. Yet, a good deal of potential value lies within the concept if we can cut through the jargon.

Essentially, reflective practice can be seen as:

- a learning conversation
- a method of accounting for ourselves
- a critical approach
- a way of interpreting the interface between practice and theory
- and a postmodernist way of knowing and learning
  (adapted from Ghaye and Ghaye, 1998).

How can you tell if you're 'doing it right'? You are reflecting when you look back on a well-planned teaching session that didn't go as well you had expected **and** when you also identify what contributed to the weaknesses of the session and what you will do about it next time. You are reflecting when you write in your learning journal about an impromptu discussion with students that worked really well **and** you also identify what contributed to the success of the session and how you can build on it next time around. You are **not** reflecting if you simply 'go over', or narrate to yourself, what you did in your teaching today – without moving forward (adapted from John Cowan, 1999).

Reflection doesn't *just* need to take place following an event, or at the end of the day. Becoming reflective means that you can use this approach as a useful, and potentially very powerful, tool at any time – before, during and after a teaching session – in order to gain benefit. We can reflect on this in Figure 5.1.

ENGAGING WITH REFLECTIVE PRACTICE

'for action'
planning carried out prior to engaging with a given situation

'in action'
responding to and acting on changes within any given situation or, put most simply, 'thinking on our feet'

'on action'
reviewing that situation and planning for what we might do next time in light of what we have learned

FIGURE 5.1 Aspects of reflective learning, based on Schön (1983, 1991)

Being able to reflect 'in action' is perhaps the most powerful of all three of these approaches as it provides you with an opportunity to react to a situation in 'real time'. However, this is a skill that develops and grows in line with your confidence as a teacher. In the following case study Lynette Matthews from Leicester University describes reflection 'in action' taking place, from her perspective as a learner herself.

Case study 5.1
THIS ISN'T WORKING...

Lynette Matthews, Leicester University

As teachers, we should all be reflective practitioners: evaluating the success of our sessions to promote student learning. However, whilst critically evaluating our practice is useful for future students as we consider how we might do something better next time, it does not help the students we have just taught. Schön (1991) advocates reflection in action whereby you are critically evaluating your practice as you are teaching. But what happens during this process when we decide that the session is not effective and indeed, not going the way we planned? What should we do?

68

Some years ago, I attended a staff development workshop run by an external facilitator, who was very experienced and knowledgeable. Half-way through his session, he announced to the predominantly seasoned academics, 'This isn't working ... Give me a moment and we'll do this a different way...' After a few minutes in deep thought, during which everyone was too stunned to do anything but sit there, he started again. At the end, all the academics found the workshop extremely useful. I suspect that this would not have been the case had the facilitator not been as courageous as he had and taken steps to remedy the situation immediately when he realised that he was confusing us. I was extremely in awe of his action and in conversations with other participants, I was not the only one.

What struck me was his commitment to ensuring that we all benefited from his workshop. Clearly he had been reading our body language throughout, which I believe is a skill often underplayed by teachers. Admittedly it can be difficult if you have large student numbers in your lectures, but reading body language can help you ascertain if your students are engaged – or even listening to you!

Perhaps we are reading our students' body language but when we sense that we are losing our students, we ignore it because we feel vulnerable. It is easier to carry on regardless but ensure that in our reflections we make notes to ensure changes for the future. However, as the very experienced facilitator had shown, it is OK to divert from the original plan during a session. It takes guts to confront the problem but it may help your learners – and if the seasoned academics are anything to judge by – students will not hold it against you.

However, a word of warning about body language; when I first started teaching in higher education, I noticed that one postgraduate student used to frown throughout my sessions. Eventually, her frown turned into a scowl and with a small group of 20 students, I could no longer ignore it so after the session I plucked up the courage to approach her about it. She broke into an apologetic smile and said, 'I do that when I am really concentrating'!

This case study highlights the benefits of being able to reflect in action in order to provide a student-centred and responsive teaching experience. If you feel that actually stopping the class and having a think would not work for you, there are other ways that you can give yourself a bit of breathing space, such as asking your students to:

- discuss a topic in pairs
- take a 5-minute break (if the timing is right)

- think about what they have learned in the class so far – and then take some responses from the floor.

The last suggestion can also help to inform your view of how the class is going and give you a steer on where it should go next. This kind of activity also helps your students to begin to engage with the process of reflection themselves. Here are some suggestions to get your students thinking reflectively.

- Ask your students to focus on their own learning journey during a class.
- Get them to establish learning goals ahead of the class and to monitor them during the session.
- End the class by asking them to review their learning goals again.
- Ensure that they understand the value of the before, in and after concepts of reflection to the learning experience.
- Think about how you might reduce the amount of content delivered during class in order to provide *space* for reflection.

(adapted from Hedberg, 2009 in Hibbert, 2013)

DEVELOPING YOUR TEACHING THROUGH REFLECTIVE PRACTICE

There are a number of frameworks that can help us to appreciate the practical value of a reflective approach. One of the most well-known is Kolb's model (1984), based on Lewin's four-stage cycle of adult learning, which recognises that development and change is a non-linear, cyclical process dependent on both our ability to learn effectively and our willingness to implement that change. Each stage of the cycle is important, influencing the degree of criticality that we are able to bring to bear on our teaching.

- *What happened?* Learning is unlikely to result from a cursory glance at some aspect of your teaching, whether it is represented to you on a student feedback form or through your own memory. We need to embody the experience in a genuinely rich fashion, perhaps in a detailed written description or commentary to a colleague.
- *How do you feel about it?* The concrete expression of the experience provides a genuine basis to observe what occurred,

enabling us to look at the experience from a variety of different angles or viewpoints, perhaps in light of a specific methodology.
- *What links can be made between practice and theory?* We may then perceive patterns and meaning within the experience, enabling us to connect the experience to concepts and theories. This richness of understanding helps us to appreciate the need for change and suggests ways forward.
- *What will you do next?* We can then employ this understanding to guide us in making changes in our practice, experimenting with new possibilities; enabling us to engage in further experiences.

The following case study from Melissa Highton, Leeds University, demonstrates how we can use Kolb's model as a structured framework to help us learn from our experiences. Also note how Melissa is actually working here with 'double loop' learning (Argyris and Schön, 1974), as she has gone through one iteration of the learning cycle already (see her comments within the context setting section), which she then follows with this cycle in order to deepen and enrich her learning – and to develop her teaching.

Case study 5.2
THE LEARNING CYCLE

Melissa Highton, University of Leeds

Context

I teach on a postgraduate module which looks at using technology in teaching. While feedback on the module in previous years has been good, comments are often characterised by conflicting views on the value of changing teaching to include new e-learning technologies. It was this feedback, and thinking about how I might respond to it, which made me rethink and plan a new approach to designing an online task for the group. The task was designed specifically to acknowledge polarisation of views and challenge participants to back up their opinions with more than anecdotal evidence.

What did you do?

I designed an online task in the shape of a formal debate on a given motion 'This house believes. . .' In this case the motion concerned the amount of time required by staff to implement technology in teaching, an issue which is of real concern to module participants. The debate lasted six weeks. The asynchronous nature of the debate online ensured that time was given to participants to prepare and reflect on postings and to gather evidence from materials covered as the module progressed. Participants were given specific roles and responsibilities and everyone in the group submitted evidence to the debate.

How did you feel about it?

In reflecting on this experience I can identify the value of the experiment on several levels. Not only was I able to respond to feedback regarding the need to recognise a range of views amongst the participants, I could also ensure that those views were expressed and challenged within the group with everyone having an equal voice. An unexpected outcome was that it was also a good classroom management tool as I was able to give specific roles to dominant characters in the group and create a place (the online debate chamber) where views could be 'heard' and recorded.

What links can be made between practice and theory?

I recognise the importance of demonstrating how examples of technology can be used in teaching and learning. In this task I was able to demonstrate how asynchronous discussion rooms can be integrated within a face-to-face module as part of a blended learning approach. Moreover, when the class were discussing the theory of designing and assessing online discussions and use of the institutional virtual learning environment, we were able to refer to what had been happening in the debate in previous weeks.

What will you do next?

The outcome has been to create a lasting resource of links and material to which participants can refer in preparing their assignments and something to which I can refer in designing the module for the following year. I plan to facilitate a similar debate – with a different motion – again.

In this case study we can see how the student feedback prompted Melissa to review and develop her teaching in a particular direction in order to better support student learning. Without the benefit of that feedback Melissa may have refocused her teaching in a way that failed to connect with her students.

Developing a more reflective approach to our practice can help us to achieve a critically evaluative stance; as can working with others. You may have received the impression so far that reflection is a solitary business but reflective practice can also involve others, and some of the richness that is required for reflective learning may result from such interactions. Reflective practice can easily become too cognitive and we need to remember that much can be gained through developing relationships with colleagues – and students – as we discuss in the following chapter, where we focus on collective practice. Seeing ourselves through our students' eyes; learning from colleagues' perceptions; creating critically reflective conversations; and team teaching as critical reflection are all ways identified by Brookfield (2017) to involve others in supporting our reflective practice. What other tools or approaches are available to us? There are some that focus more on a rational approach, which carefully analyses practice or plans for subsequent practice, while others allow learning to emerge in a more open fashion. Some tools focus on the written word while other approaches focus on dialogue. Perhaps you are the kind of person who reflects best when taking some exercise, that re-energises you physically as well as mentally. Going for a walk and mulling over a critical incident, or popping out to a coffee shop to jot down a few notes, can all contribute to your development as an effective reflective practitioner.

To get you started, we're going to look at a range of tools to support reflection and learning (but don't limit yourself to these – explore the literature and find the approach that best suits you and your practice):

- assumption hunting
- use of lenses to interrogate practice
- keeping a learning log or journal
- learning from peer observation.

Assumption hunting (Brookfield, 2017) involves consciously adopting a critically reflective stance towards the underpinnings of your practice. 'Assumptions are the taken-for-granted beliefs about the world and our place within it that guide our actions' (ibid.: 5). The idea is to hunt down your assumptions or the aspects of your practice that you take for granted, such as presumptions about what constitutes 'good' teaching or strategies that support student learning. This can also mean putting our ideas about innovative learning approaches to the 'assumptions test', as discussed in this case study by Isabella Chaney, from Royal Holloway, University of London.

Case study 5.3
GETTING THE MESSAGE ACROSS

Isabella Chaney, Royal Holloway, University of London

I teach and manage a transnational undergraduate programme my UK university has in Singapore. The programme is a combination of face-to-face teaching and a distance learning component using Moodle. For the first three years of the programme I recorded ten one-hour lectures each with Power Point presentations that students could listen to and watch via Moodle. I thought this was a helpful way for students to supplement the face-to-face teaching and readings and as they could be viewed in their own time there should be a strong take-up by busy students.

After a couple of years of running the course I noticed that there were only a handful of students looking at the videoed lectures. My initial thoughts were that they were too boring and so students preferred to just attend the face-to-face sessions and do the course readings. It was rather disappointing as I had put in a lot of effort trying to make the videos and PowerPoints engaging and I had hoped it would be useful as 'extra' support.

At the next student-staff committee I asked for feedback on the videos and queried whether there was any reason students were not using them as a study aid. I was told that many students in Singapore do not have a one-hour block of time free to watch the videos. There are two main reasons for the lack of time: many are working to support their education, and many are responsible for the care of family members. The latter is not only in terms of dependent children but also of older family members. For many, their elderly parents and grandparents live in the same household and the students are required to assist in caring duties as is the norm in Asian culture.

Therefore, it was evident that students did not have time to sit down and take in the one-hour video material. What they needed were bite-sized videos with short and focused messages. So the one-hour lectures were then changed to 10–15 minute maximum length videos that were not the standard lecture but instead required the student to have read either a case study, a journal article or a 'hot' topic from business publications prior to watching the video. The video content is a critical discussion of the case or articles. Students feel more engaged with this method of delivery as the shortness of the video means they can fit it more easily into their life. They also appreciate the fact that they can do the readings and then see if they have fully understood the various arguments of what they have read by watching my video discussions. What

I learnt from this is that it is important to work with students by listening to their needs, and not to make assumptions about what these might be – however well intentioned! – and to adjust teaching delivery methods to 'get the message across' in ways that are relevant and useful to our students' learning.

This case study raises a number of issues relating to the use of innovative teaching methods and the importance of understanding and responding to cultural learning contexts. Innovation takes time and effort. Don't assume that because students don't make use of a resource that it is boring or useless – it may need to be re-purposed.

Try assumption hunting for yourself. Draw up a list of teaching-related issues about which you think you may already hold assumptions e.g. it would be impossible to introduce interactive teaching methods into my lecture class of over 100 students.

1. Consider your list. Now look beyond these immediate responses – what do you find underneath? e.g. *I don't think my students would respond to interactive teaching methods in the lecture setting and I might lose control of the class.*
2. Check the validity of your assumptions by discussing them with colleagues e.g. *what experiences have your colleagues had in making their teaching more interactive when working with large groups.*
3. Check the validity of your assumptions again by observing your students more closely, talking with them and implementing alternative teaching and learning strategies e.g. *try introducing some pair work or small group problem solving within some of your lectures. What worked well and what could have been improved? Ask your students!*

p.s. Continue to check your assumptions on a regular basis!

(adapted from Zachary, 2000)

Our assumptions can colour our everyday practice even though we advocate different attitudes and approaches. Argyris and Schön's (1974) seminal work acknowledged this situation by referring to our 'espoused theories' versus our 'theories in use'. Argyris and Schön argued that we all have 'mental maps' which guide us in our actions in any given situation, and that these can be quite different to the theories that we say we follow. For example, we might attempt to rationalise our behaviour by drawing on a theoretical perspective, let's say our use of lecturing as the mainstay of our teaching practice, which we argue relates to effective working with large classes. However, our theory in use might be quite different, in that we use lecturing as our only teaching methodology because we are too busy and stressed to think about what else we might do with a large group of students. Smith (2001) argues that reflection has a key role to play here in revealing the theory in use and in exploring the way in which it relates to our espoused theory. The gap in itself does not pose a problem – unless it grows too large – but a connection between the two 'creates a dynamic for reflection and for dialogue'. Such 'double-loop' learning arises from developing an in-depth awareness and knowledge about what we think and how we act. Consequently, assumption hunting has a key role to play in our practice when we encounter any new teaching and learning situation. It can also be an enlightening exercise to carry out *with* your students.

Using lenses to interrogate practice is a concept described throughout this book and specifically referred to again in Chapter 7, looking at drivers to change our teaching and Chapter 10, understanding teaching excellence. It's a powerful approach that allows us to take a critical look at our practice by adopting a particular perspective and specific stance, rather than just simply through our own eyes. Using several lenses together – in order to triangulate a particular issue – provides multiple perspectives. Stephen Brookfield's (2017) four lenses of critical reflection are:

- students' eyes
- colleagues' perceptions
- theory
- personal experience.

Review point 5.1
TAKE A LENS TO YOUR TEACHING

Consider what other kinds of lenses might be relevant and useful for you to use to interrogate your practice. For example:

- disciplinary expectations
- institutional learning and teaching strategy
- inclusive curriculum approach
- internationalisation policy.

In the following case study, Janet Lord from Manchester Metropolitan University, describes how engaging with the idea of Brookfield's lenses helped her to reflect on a teaching challenge and to develop her teaching in a way that put her learners at the centre.

Case study 5.4
LEARNING THROUGH LENSES

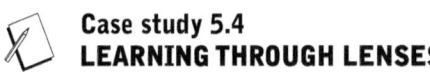

Janet Lord, Manchester Metropolitan University

After a teaching session on Social Justice I was feeling despondent. This was a group of students in a large urban university in the North of England and they weren't living lives of privilege, very far from it; but my critique of meritocracy hadn't hit the spot. The point I was trying to make had really passed them by. What I was doing so far with this group wasn't working. For years I have kept a reflective journal. It's been a way of thinking for me – I write to think, especially when I need clarity. As a teacher educator, I've found that when students want to improve their teaching, it's helpful to use the work of Brookfield (1998; 2017) on reflective lenses. It felt as if it was now time to get my journal out and to use Brookfield's work again myself.

Brookfield's 'lenses' are designed to provide multiple perspectives on who we are and what we do and they can help us to take informed actions. These are the lenses and this is what they led me to think.

The first lens is **'the eyes of students'**. I needed to think about how students saw me, and about the power dynamic in the classroom. I decided to use Brookfield's idea of 'the muddiest point' – asking why it wasn't clear for them that the notion of meritocracy didn't reflect the realities of life. And it soon became clear that the students felt discouraged as by suggesting that hard work wasn't enough, I was undermining their identity. '*So there's no point in someone like me working at all is there?',* one said. Without realising, I was sabotaging my own teaching and the way I had tried to build their self-confidence.

When I looked through **the lens of my own autobiography as a learner and teacher**, I realised that I had enjoyed challenging students by suggesting that meritocracy did not exist. However, in doing this I was in fact disempowering them by undermining their whole sense of being. The way I was going about it was all wrong.

To use the lens of **colleagues' experiences and ideas**, I talked to teachers who taught similar topics to similar kinds of students. One suggestion was that

I should consider challenging the students more gently, so that they understood the intellectual argument before they moved on to consider its personal implications. One way to do it; I hadn't thought of that.

And so to **literature and theory** as the final lens. I read again the literature that connects ideas about social justice to identity: I looked in more depth at work on critical pedagogy.

That led to my thinking about how I could improve my teaching; by starting from a different position, by moving students gradually away from their entrenched positions, by empowering. I created activities that looked at diversity and inequality, that built on students' existing understandings. It worked; there were some 'aha' moments, and suddenly they 'got it'. Students were surprised at the inequality they were seeing, but felt less personally exposed, and so understood better.

My journal had been of use; I learned about myself, my teaching and about a process of improvement. I'll use that journal again.

Keeping a **learning log or journal,** as highlighted in the last case study, can help you to reflect on your practice over a longer period of time. This approach to developing your teaching can support you in reviewing where you were in relation to your practice at a particular time, how far you have developed, and what strategies or approaches supported that development. You can also reflect on why your practice has developed in a particular way or style, or why it has not developed as much as you had planned or differently from what you had anticipated. In order to maintain the momentum, keep the entries concise. Use drawings, diagrams or bullet point lists – anything that makes the exercise maintainable and meaningful for you. In order to get started you might think about working around a structure such as:

- what happened?
- what did I learn from that incident?
- how have I been able to apply that learning to my practice?

On beginning a course on teaching and learning you might find it useful to keep such a log which will allow you to review your progress over the course of your studies. In your first year of teaching a new module, or taking on a new postgraduate student to supervise, or planning a distance learning course you might consider keeping a log. This could include details of your teaching or planning, your thoughts on how the sessions went or how your ideas are progressing – and what you might do the next time that you have to give that particular lecture, engage with your next supervision session, or have to think about delivering that complex topic in a stimulating and interesting way. Regardless of how experienced we become as teachers there is always value in maintaining some form of log, perhaps to capture a special moment or to record your response to a challenging situation. We think that we will remember these important events but it is all too easy for them to slip away unnoticed amidst our hectic lives.

Peer observation – or review - of your teaching often forms an element of teaching and learning programmes, where both your tutor and peer learners may be involved in the observations; and then as part of ongoing continuing professional development. It should be viewed positively rather than as something to be endured or 'got through'. Actively seek it out if it is not forthcoming. In the following case study, one of us explains the impact that peer observation has had on the development of our teaching practice.

Case study 5.5
'CAN I OBSERVE YOUR TEACHING?'

I can remember every one of my early career peer observations. The first was as a postgraduate tutor and I thought I'd done not too badly. The students were keen to support me and it seemed to go OK – but I remember getting very tongue-tied and confused during the de-brief when my observer picked up on the all things I hadn't done so well and I left that experience somewhat deflated. It didn't help that the observer was also one of my PhD supervisors, so I already felt under the microscope. The second observation was of one of my lectures in my new role as a Teaching Fellow. The observer sat in the middle of the lecture theatre; he looked bored throughout. At the end of the session he said it had been OK. My third observation was as a participant on my PG Cert in teaching course; and this time it was videoed! I don't remember anything about the feedback but I do remember watching the video and being horrified at the way in which I marched back and forth across the front of the lecture theatre, looking stern and determined. I scared myself, never mind the students.

As I now team teach almost everything I do in front of a class I feel that there is an ongoing process of peer support of teaching and I regularly ask for feedback and advice – it has become second nature to my teaching activity. However, those early experiences taught me a lot of things about the process as much as the outcome:

- Consider the power balance between observer and the person being observed. Are there likely to be any issues? Will it be seen more as an assessment of ability rather than a tool to enhance practice?
- As an observer, always provide something of substance that the person being observed can take away from the session. If it's just 'OK', why is that? What went well – and what could have been better?
- Video can be a very powerful tool but use it carefully. Images can stay with an individual much longer than words but they need to be supported by guidance, support and challenge.

Observation of teaching is a developmental process so you should focus on how you can build on the positive aspects of your practice and consider the ways in which you can develop the weaker areas. Find out what your observer is looking for. As with any assessment, the criteria should be transparent and available to you. Some of the criteria may cover aspects of a teaching session that have not occurred to you before, and you may want to flag up to the observer that you are unsure of the extent of your ability in these areas, and that you would particularly appreciate feedback on them. This is not a sign of incompetence but rather a clear signal to your observer that you are aware of both your stronger and weaker areas and that you see the observation as a good opportunity to develop your teaching.

Don't be tempted to pick your 'best' class for the observation. The aim is not to achieve the ideal teaching session but rather to demonstrate your ability to react to and work with the class, regardless of their level of ability. Much better to be able to demonstrate your strategies for motivating disinterested students than having the 'perfect' class. Having said that, however, it would be prudent not to choose a class where only one or two students ever turn up or which centres around a presentation from a student with a notoriously poor attendance rate. Those are issues that can be dealt with at another time! Once you have reassured your students that the observer is not there to assess their performance but yours, they do tend to react very positively and supportively. Nonetheless, having another person in your class, particularly in a non-participatory observer's role, will change the dynamic so be prepared for perhaps less banter or light-hearted exchanges from the students; but potentially more effort!

The feedback that you receive from your teaching observation will hopefully be constructive and supportive. However, we should not forget that providing good feedback, centred around constructive criticism, is a skill in itself. Be discriminating. You are dealing here with the values and attitudes of others. They might 'see' things within your teaching that perhaps resonate with potential development areas within their own practice, meaning that they unconsciously project those feelings onto you. Always take time to review and discuss feedback – don't react spontaneously without giving it due consideration, perhaps asking for a second opinion from another colleague, or situating your practice within an understanding of the relevant theory. Most importantly, create an action plan. It is important to do this as soon as possible after reviewing the feedback, particularly if you will not be teaching that class, module or course for another year.

Review point 5.2
ENGAGING WITH PEER REVIEW

- Think about how you might get more out of the observation process to help you develop your teaching.

- Gaining multiple perspectives on your practice provides excellent triangulation – and links to Brookfield's lenses again.

- Consider making a video recording of your teaching session. This can be particularly useful in that it constitutes a permanent record of practice which can be revisited and reviewed, not only by you yourself, but also in conjunction with a mentor, buddy or close colleague.

CONCLUSIONS

Becoming reflective is also about becoming critical. It's about taking our experiences and learning from them in a way that is interrogative but always forward-looking. It's about working with others to gain multiple perspectives on what we do and how we are as teachers. It's about stretching and challenging ourselves to become reflexive and to recognise and acknowledge 'the most deeply hidden influences and constraints: those hidden within our own assumptions' (Hibbert, 2013: 804). Our final case study in this chapter, from Fiona Kennedy, Glasgow Caledonian University, demonstrates how reflecting on her experiences as a learner helped her to revisit a topic that she had struggled with as a student, in order to deliver the same material more effectively and engagingly when she came to teach it herself, and in order to enhance and develop her teaching.

Case study 5.6
DON'T LOSE THE LEARNING

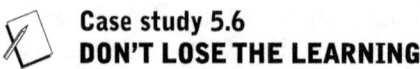

Fiona Kennedy, Glasgow Caledonian University

I never liked anatomy when I studied it as part of my Occupational Therapy education. It bored me, and the idea of learning the origin, insertion, nerve supply, blood supply and action of every muscle filled me with little more than apathy! Lectures were didactic and practical classes involved looking at dissections of human cadavers in a laboratory setting. The sterile learning environment left me uninterested. Quite apart from anything else, I anticipated working with people who were alive and moving!

When I entered higher education as a new lecturer, one of the first subjects I was asked to teach was anatomy. My heart sank until I realised that I was being given the opportunity to revisit and reflect on the teaching strategies and move away from the didactic experience of learning that I had experienced myself. Working with a colleague, I set about trying to make anatomy classes as interactive and professionally contextualised as possible. We worked with the students simulating the kind of everyday activities that might be seen within therapeutic practice, within and around the classroom setting (e.g. making a hot drink; walking up and down stairs; getting dressed; transferring in and out of a car; and even playing games such as Twister and Jenga). By engaging in these activities, students could feel the movement within their own bodies, and observe the movement on their peers. This helped them to identify, visualise and often feel where specific muscles were situated, and to understand the relationship between muscles and movements as components of everyday tasks.

We talked with students about their activities outwith university and then set them homework tasks of analysing their movements while doing grocery shopping, climbing aboard buses and catching up with friends over a coffee. This encouraged students to think about their learning after the class, and they told us stories of thinking so much about their anatomy whilst in the supermarket, that they forgot items from their shopping lists! We helped them to create formative assessments for their peers by working in small groups to make quizzes and crosswords (based on muscle names and movements) and then posted these as revision tools for the rest of their class.

The student response to the interactive nature of the classes was extremely positive – they enjoyed the experiential nature of their learning and could explain how they would use their knowledge in a professional context. Their engagement in classes and their enthusiasm to learn was not the only measure of success; their readiness for assessment was also notable, with 100 per cent pass rates across the subject not being uncommon. Further still, as teaching staff, my colleagues and I thoroughly enjoyed the experience and were more than happy to teach anatomy in following years! Far from being the subject that I loathed when I was a student myself, anatomy became a real pleasure to teach.

Don't lose the learning.

 REFERENCES

Argyris, C. & Schön, D. (1974). *Theory in Practice: Increasing Professional Effectiveness*. San Francisco: Jossey-Bass.

Brookfield, S. (1998). Critically reflective practice. *Journal of Continuing Education in the Health Professions*, *18*, 197 – 205.

Brookfield, S. (2017). *Becoming a Critically Reflective Teacher* (2nd edition). San Francisco: Jossey-Bass.

Cowan, J. (1999). *On Becoming an Innovative University Teacher: Reflection in Action*. Buckingham: SRHE/OUP.

Ghaye, A. & Ghaye, K. (1998). *Teaching and Learning through Critical Reflective Practice*. London: David Fulton.

Hibbert, P. (2013). Approaching reflexivity through critical reflection: Issues for critical management education. *Journal of Management Education*, 37(6), 803 – 27.

Kolb, D. A. (1984). *Experiential Learning: Experience as the Source of Learning and Development.* New Jersey: Prentice-Hall.

Schön, D. (1983). *The Reflective Practitioner.* San Francisco: Jossey-Bass.

Schön, D. (1991). *The Reflective Practitioner: How Professionals Think in Action.* Aldershot: Ashgate.

Smith, M. K. (2001). Chris Argyris: theories of action, double-loop learning and organizational learning. *The Encyclopedia of Informal Education.* www.infed.org/thinkers/argyris.htm [Online, accessed 30 August 2018]

Zachary, L. (2000). *The Mentor's Guide: Facilitating Effective Learning Relationships.* San Francisco: Jossey-Bass.

Chapter 6

Shifting collective practice

INTRODUCTION

Working with others has become a cornerstone of academic life. Colleagues, peers and students all play a role in shaping our teaching practice. We work in a teaching and learning environment that is increasingly focused on team effort, interdisciplinary working, subject-related networks and sharing of practice. Some of these groupings appear to come 'ready-made' while others have to be created and supported through networking, and the development of peer groups and contacts. All of them have to be nurtured and maintained. The growing importance of the collective in the life of the Academy mirrors wider changes in society, where networks have increasingly come to shape our world. Castells (2010), indeed, has suggested that the information technology paradigm has come to ensure that networks pervade our society.

This means that many enhancements to teaching are taken forward by a group of colleagues. After all, an entire programme of study is hardly ever offered by a single lecturer. If you are looking for a step change in the calibre of your teaching, then the way forward is likely to involve plenty of work in common with others. And it is also the case that more students are also likely to be affected by an enhancement as colleagues are drawn in, so that your impact is greater. If you want to make a splash as a teacher, then leading on a change in collective practice will mean that others are keenly aware of your contribution, something that would not be so apparent if you had just enhanced your own world.

We saw in Chapter 3 how a discipline provides a focus for people to come together in order to enhance their teaching. It remains the case, however, that staff engaged in teaching come together in many different ways. Perhaps you are in a department that spans several disciplines or working on a teaching innovation with colleagues in another faculty or university. Or it might be the case that the intellectual horizons for your teaching are shaped by the networks that you maintain through social media. This chapter thus takes a look at how we can connect with each other in order to improve teaching. What does it take to convince a critical mass of colleagues that an enhancement is worth progressing together?

FOCI FOR COLLECTIVE PRACTICE

If we are to understand how to enhance collective practices it is important to understand the basis on which members of staff come together. There are, of course, many foci for this to occur, but wishful thinking that colleagues will just see the light and follow your initiative is not usually one of them. It often takes something quite substantial to move the deep-seated attitudes that determine which teaching practices are undertaken. It will make sense, then, to start this chapter by looking further at possible foci around which those teaching in universities tend to pull together.

Life is organised on an institutional basis. We saw earlier in the book how attitudes and behaviours of staff are shaped by institutional logics – a mindset, as it were, that is common to staff working in the given organisation. Institutional strategies are ubiquitous as institutions seek to climb league tables or improve their performance relative to competitors. The institutional strategy offers an immediate reason to pull together. Take a look at your institution's strategy. How does it relate to your own interests or to what you think your students value? What needs does it highlight to which you and your colleagues are genuinely committed?

A new building, refurbished laboratory or revamped design studio all offer an occasion to adjust the nature of the practices that are carried out within them. The possibilities for interdisciplinary working amongst students are strictly limited if each discipline has its own separate suite of laboratories, located in different buildings. But what if a set of disciplines share common laboratory space? One of our own institutions (Liverpool) now has a shared central laboratory for students across the physical, environmental and archaeological sciences. Staff from different disciplines will meet each other in meetings or in the corridors. Their discussions range over far more than just agreeing the timetable or common safety procedures. And what better way to prepare students for interdisciplinary research or development during subsequent careers in industry or academia?

Research provides another reason to come together. There is good scope, indeed, for innovation in teaching on the basis of research groups. Laidlaw (2003) describes how discussions within a research group in

SHIFTING COLLECTIVE PRACTICE

Computer Science at Brown University, Rhode Island, led to a collaboration with the Illustration Department at Rhode Island School of Design. The initiative brought together students from backgrounds in computer science and design to create software in an immersive virtual environment. Strong research groups often provide a basis for reframing how an area of study could be approached. New modules can often be conceptualised on the basis of research agendas, and new degree programmes often arise from them. Are there ways in which your own research with others could provide the basis for a new module or degree programme?

Threats from the outside environment are a powerful focus for staff to come together, as Gibbs, Knapper and Piccinin (2008) highlighted in a classic study of teaching excellence in research-intensive departments. A damning report from a quality review of the department might have highlighted specific areas that need to change. Lower than hoped-for recruitment often means that staff members who leave are not replaced in a hurry, if at all. In what ways could your courses be made more suited to the aspirations and interests of potential students? Kahn (2014) argued that it is the concerns that matter to students that play a key role in enabling them to take responsibility for their learning. Are there any immediate threats to the standing or future of your own department or school? How could you adapt your collective practice in ways that would enable you to address these threats?

Courses with a heavy online element to them, or that are offered fully online, are typically developed on a basis that is strongly collective. After all, you are likely in these cases to have learning technologists, librarians and other colleagues working with you. Given the complexity of curriculum development in this area, there are increasing numbers of people in support roles. Povl Götke and his colleagues in Case study 6.1 demonstrate the steps they have taken to create a specialist team in order to better support their students' learning.

Case study 6.1
DEVELOPING THE SPECIALIST TEAM

Povl Götke, Jens Dam and Gina Bay, Teaching and Learning Centre,
University of Southern Denmark

Unplanned, unstructured and random, team teaching can be the result of an ad hoc getting together of like-minded colleagues. We have tried another approach, however, where we have put a team together built upon a range of different strengths and backgrounds. With an academic leading the curriculum development, and two librarians with responsibility for the e-learning platform and electronic information searching, we set up our new programme.

Students were organised into small groups and were assigned a task to be solved where they had to address a number of requirements – for example, everyone had to include at least three articles in their answer and to organise their co-operative working via an e-learning platform. What was important here was that all the groups received support and advice from a subject specialist. Librarians advised on the task of searching for information and articles, and guidance with e-learning enabled the collaborative development of a specialised professional database where working papers, notes, links and references could be deposited.

The advantage of taking this approach to teaching is that every single member of the team provides a valuable, specialised contribution to the overall picture. It provides a more organic and unified structure to team teaching, which is also challenging and rewarding, where individuals cannot avoid relating to, reflecting on, discussing and developing the team itself in support of student learning.

Undoubtedly the bringing together of individuals within the team who represented the educational and instructional side of things, combined with the information retrieval and e-learning skills of the librarians, was a great advantage to the successful development of such a programme. While these individuals, and the sections of the academic community that they represent, are traditionally closely related, the structured integration provided by the team demonstrated the strength of a multi-disciplinary approach in supporting student learning.

Curriculum development is an ongoing feature of university life, although perhaps more so in some disciplines rather than others! We regularly see new or revised programmes of study, and these need to be agreed upon. Students quite reasonably expect to see some consistency in the different elements of their programmes of study. Jessop and Tomas (2017) have suggested that a programme-wide approach to assessment offers an excellent basis on which to generate significant improvements in student learning. It seems, for instance, that too much summative assessment can easily lead students to narrowly focus on securing high grades, at the expense of more imaginative approaches to learning. When revising or developing a programme, you might follow a methodology that deliberately brings staff together as an integral part of the process, as occurs in Gilly Salmon's *carpe diem* learning design workshops (Salmon, Ross, Pechenkina, and Chase, 2015) or the process that the Transforming the Experience of Students through Assessment (TESTA) project employs to bring together lecturers, students and others in establishing an evidence base for programme-level change, and in then using that evidence base to develop or redevelop a programme (Jessop, El-Hakim, and Gibbs, 2011).

Resources are often shared across a department or even a discipline. Teaching resources take significant time to develop, as we will see later in this chapter with Case study 6.3. If everyone begins to share their resources with each other, perhaps through a networked drive or a cloud file-sharing service, then there is good scope for one person's ideas to influence the practices of their colleagues. What resources would helpfully support your own colleagues? What institutional or departmental mechanisms are in place for you to share resources with each other? Why not set up an online location to share resources with your colleagues. You might consult with an e-learning specialist before taking the idea too far.

These ideas offer a selection of foci around which staff come together, but there are many many more. Teaching often occurs in teams and many aspects of the process of assessing students (and awarding degrees to them) need to be agreed collectively. Student support provides further occasions to work together, and there is a good deal to be gained when a resident tutor and others help animate student life in a hall of residence. The list goes on. Recognising the collective basis of your teaching offers a sound basis on which to develop your teaching.

THE CENTRALITY OF RELATIONSHIPS

Awareness of the foci around which colleagues pull together is one thing, but finding yourself in a position to propose an enhancement and see it through are something quite different. What the different foci for work together that we considered in the previous section open is the scope to engage in conversation with others about your work together. Other people will have their own concerns about what is going on, and what could be done differently. You have an opportunity to see how well your own concerns align with those of your colleagues. You might be persuaded by their concerns, and see ways in which these now common concerns could be addressed. Change can go in different directions. You might find yourself adopting your colleagues' practices! What this does mean, though, is that if a sharing of concerns is to occur it will help to know your colleagues well. Before we move on to looking at delivering on a shift in collective practice, it will help to look at networking.

In the first instance, capacity for development is determined by your network of relationships, as Gustavsen (2001) has argued. Colleagues provide insights into the political agenda of those whose approval is needed, knowledge of existing practice on the area, resources, ideas, stakeholders, team members delivering the change, and so on. It is hard to over-emphasise how much difference a robust network can make to developing your teaching. Hectic teaching schedules, endless meetings, marking, deadlines and piles of paperwork. These are only some of the reasons, however, that can prevent you from interacting and networking with your colleagues.

Networking is important to everyone's career development but it can be particularly important if, for example, you are on a part-time or fixed-term contract; your office is not centrally located on campus; or you spend a lot of time working independently, when it can be all too easy to be missed out of the information loop. Begin to think about the role that networking plays in your working life by considering these review questions.

- Consider the people you have contact with in your professional life. Which would you regard as your immediate circle and what function do these individuals play in your working life?
- What about the next circle? And the next?
- How many circles are there?
- Are you aware of whether the circles overlap – and is this important to you?
- Do you actively seek out new networks and acquaintances?
- How can you do this better?

When people start to discuss networking they often think automatically of conferences and the associated costs – and they can feel overwhelmed. Conferences can be great for networking if you make best use of the opportunities, but there are many ways to network effectively. The opportunities are there to attend seminars, staff development sessions or institutional events, to join reading groups, the sports centre or a musical society, or to build social media usage into your working day, and so on. Networking can be as simple as inviting a colleague out to coffee or lunch, and finding out about their actual interests. There are many

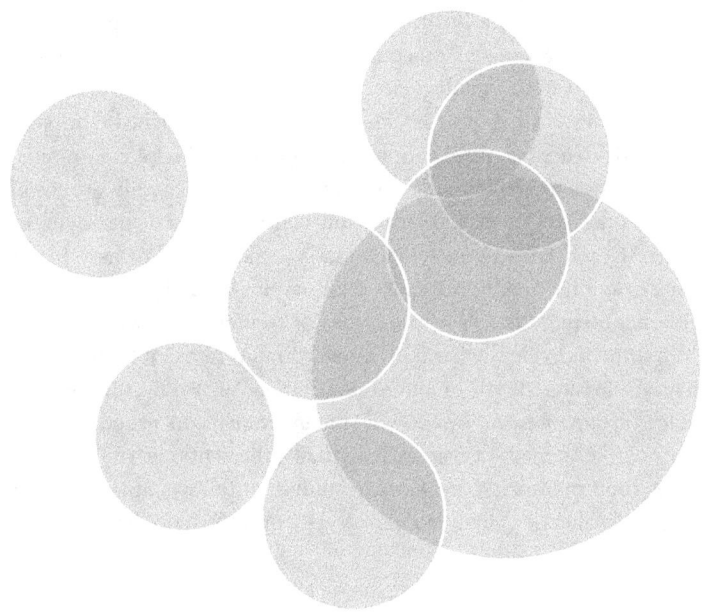

■ **FIGURE 6.1** A review of your professional networks

levels at which you can begin to network. Getting a mentor, for instance, doesn't just mean adding one person to your network – mentoring usually leads to introductions to others. If you have a close relationship with someone then they will usually be willing to recommend you to others, and to take action on your behalf. Even still, conference attendance can involve far more than just presenting:

- Take a look at the delegate list and see who you might connect with. There may be good value in missing sessions so that you can chat informally with other participants – perhaps colleagues you've not seen for a while.
- After attending a conference, send a brief email to everyone that you would like to keep in contact with.

There is a lot to be said for networking that leads to substantive relationships with others, and not just an occasional coffee at conferences. Cross-cutting teaching roles (e.g. on employability or inclusion) give you

SHIFTING COLLECTIVE PRACTICE

access to a wider view on institutional life, as do staff development sessions or institutional events. You could run a session at one of these yourself. One good way to establish close relationships with a more diverse set of colleagues is to engage in action learning. This might be in place on your initial teaching qualification, but regional or disciplinary opportunities are often available. Action learning sets are essentially groups of critical friends who meet to discuss and consider a particular issue or concern. At each meeting one individual has the chance to have his or her issue examined and discussed in detail within the action learning set. As with mentoring, the role of the set is not to immediately offer advice and to tell the individual what they should do, but rather it is to explore the issue in greater depth by open questioning, providing support and challenge throughout, and by allowing the individual concerned to arrive at their own, informed, decisions. Essentially, the action learning set is a form of group mentoring. In the case study that follows Stuart Mackay discusses the value he gained from involvement in an action learning set.

Case study 6.2
SEE THE WORLD AS OTHERS SEE IT

Stuart Mackay, Directorate of Radiography, University of Salford

I took part in an action learning set for a period of three years. This involved meeting with a group of seven people once a fortnight to support each other as we each undertook a project related to both our work and an educational qualification. Being together with the same people over a long period of time built up trust and familiarity and produced a very supportive and nurturing environment. Working on a work-related project meant that we often brought issues to the set which were familiar problems to us all.

Over time we were able to communicate very effectively and share our underpinning emotions. Emerging from this experience was a fantastic opportunity to 'see the world as others see it'. This led to the insight that actually, I was not really that different to many of my colleagues!! We often experienced the same powerful motivating forces such as fear of failure, not wanting to make a fool of oneself, anxiety, and fatigue. Such factors have a powerful moderating effect on the way we behave and hence the way we appear to others. This realisation enabled me to feel closer to other teachers and learners and to understand others' behaviour more. I became more tolerant of others and looked to see how they might be seeing the world. For example I observed a colleague chairing a meeting poorly. Instead of feeling angry or that this meeting was a waste of my time I soon realised it was because they were feeling anxious about their performance as Chair. I worked on trying to reduce the individual's anxiety by pointing out the positive aspects of their chairing technique so that next time they might feel less anxious and perform better. So this key learning point helped me to understand and work with my colleagues in a more effective way.

So I believe one of the most important ways of developing my practice is to try and get to know people as individuals and realise that we all have very similar motivating forces to our behaviour. Trying to 'see the world as others see it' helps to keep me rooted in a reality shared with other teachers and learners.

Consider the possibilities that we have raised in this section, and make a commitment to act on at least one of them!

SEEING IT THROUGH

Awareness of the possibilities and relationships with one's colleagues are one thing, but there is a time for action. There is always a risk involved in trying something new; will it work? Introducing a development takes you outside your comfort zone, almost by definition. At the very outset some confidence is required; you need to hold your nerve! Confidence is, though, only an initial requirement: it helps to have an appreciation for the development process (see for instance Kahn and Baume, 2003). This forms a key element in your ability to carry a development through to its conclusion.

There will be plenty of things that you could do – the skill in developing education is to pick an initiative that has a realistic chance of making it. Four considerations are particularly significant:

- ■ Setting a clear aim for your development – at the outset it is important to be clear what you are trying to achieve. What is the challenge for students or teachers that you are seeking to address?
- ■ Understanding of the needs of all those involved – this understanding will come in part from your own experience, but it may also draw on a more formal analysis of the needs, perhaps informed by student feedback or even focus groups.

- Awareness of the activity that others have already carried out – there is a growing body of case studies on development in higher education, as we have already seen in Chapter 2. It clearly makes sense to carry out a review of the literature, and relevant practice before embarking on the design. This can include taking a look at relevant educational theory, to provide a framework to understand and shape the development, reducing reliance on trial and error. Drawing on this prior work more fully might well help to reduce your sense of uncertainty as you embark on something new.
- A rich vein of ideas on which to draw – this enables you to select the most promising ideas as a basis for the development, increasing your chances of success. Ideas do not appear from nowhere, but are often triggered by exchanges with others (again, see Gustavsen, 2001).

The design of the development should respect such considerations, rather than simply be invented from scratch, otherwise you may well run into difficulty. For instance, if you simply jump in with a 'good idea', and immediately invent your teaching materials, you may find your development is irrelevant after all to your students' needs. This initial assessment of what is worth developing provides a clear basis for overall design of the development.

Addressing these considerations will help ensure that your development is fit for purpose, but a development project also involves introducing change into an existing environment, and it is thus important to take into account the factors that will support or hinder your new initiative when it comes to implementation. The idea itself may be an excellent one, but other factors will also determine whether it can be successfully implemented in practice. The complexity of higher education means that adaptations will often be required to your initial plans, and these need to be possible.

Review point 6.1
SELECTING A DEVELOPMENT

Identify two areas that are ripe for a shift in collective practice. Assess their relative merits against the analysis offered in this chapter. Is there anything that will help to provide a focus around which you can come together?

SHIFTING COLLECTIVE PRACTICE

On a personal level, motivation is certainly essential, and is likely to be enhanced if you can use the development for more than one purpose. You might use a development project as a way to take forward your own teaching, and thus to enhance your students' educational experiences; but it could also count towards assessment on a programme in learning and teaching; you can use it to secure funding, to develop further expertise, as evidence for a promotion, or to develop stronger relationships with colleagues. This can all help you to develop and sustain high levels of self-efficacy, the belief that you can achieve what you set out to do (Schwarzer, 2014). It is surprising how much difference self-efficacy makes to student learning, as the meta-analysis by Richardson, Abraham and Bond (2012) demonstrated. Indeed, the study suggested that, after working towards goals for one's grades, self-efficacy was the next most significant influence on student achievement. The situation is different when it comes to catalysing change amongst colleagues, of course, but it is essential nonetheless.

You will need to involve colleagues in delivering your initiative, and they will have to be on board; is that actually likely to be the case? It is particularly important to assess the likely contribution of your colleagues, given that they can either provide assistance at key points or create barriers to progress on the project. The approval of managers or committee chairs may well also be needed for a development to go ahead. Is this likely to be forthcoming? If the point is to come together in collective practice, then the way in which you take forward the initiative should respect this. Hilary Rollin explores in Case study 6.3 how shared resources should be just that, shared resources.

Case study 6.3
ENGAGING COLLEAGUES IN A DEVELOPMENT

Hilary Rollin, Department of Modern Languages, Oxford Brookes University

So you are all set to produce some brilliant new materials that colleagues will have to use? Excellent; but before you start thumping the keyboard in the wee small hours, take a step back. Try to recall how it felt when a colleague approached you in a state of euphoria with some hot-off-the-press materials, and all you had to do was deliver them to an enraptured class.

Might it have been a rather less enthralling experience than I have just suggested? Did you feel threatened at being confronted with new materials?

SHIFTING COLLECTIVE PRACTICE

Did they seem semi-digested, and not in line with the learning outcomes? Riddled with infelicities of style? Were they idiosyncratic, a departure from the 'normal' sequence, and hard to follow? Was the approach frankly wacky? Did it savour of innovation for its own sake? Most of us can readily identify with such scenarios.

I can recall instances when the materials which a colleague produced for me to deliver reached me allowing insufficient preparation time, such as the occasions when they appeared under the door part-way through a two-hour class. That they appeared before the end of the class was perhaps a triumph on the part of my colleague, but did not contribute to my equanimity. Not only that, but the materials were so inordinately clever that I had difficulty understanding them, let alone being able to explain them to the students. We often learn through our teaching, but feeling mystified about a text or a technique is not a sound basis for gaining the confidence of one's students. I nonetheless survived, as did they.

Of course we all want our colleagues to report back that the class that hitherto has always had them in despair has been transformed into a roaring success, all due to our inspired materials. This might conceivably happen, or it might not. However, it is more likely to occur if we can avoid colleagues delivering our materials with hesitation and embarrassment.

The way to helping colleagues take ownership of materials, other than producing the goods on time, is consulting them, and involving them in the process. Not only is that likely to help them view your materials positively, it is likely to give people space to think them through. You may even find they provide you with feedback, coming up with ideas you can incorporate, or maybe their eagle eye can enable you to purge the materials of some of those otherwise embarrassing typos and non-sequiturs. Your colleagues may well then trial the materials from a position of involvement.

This is the joyous side of teamwork; at this point, you, the proud creator step back after hours of hard labour, and hear your colleague explain to others the intricacies of the materials you slaved over for hours, and for which he/she contributed a few minor adjustments. Lips sealed, you listen to your colleague taking the credit. But isn't that what you wanted, to get your colleague involved?

It is centrally important to effective working together that everyone involved in the team is regarded as a real member of that team; this should include graduate tutors and support staff who may normally only

SHIFTING COLLECTIVE PRACTICE

be included at the end stages of team planning in order to run tutorials, pick up routine assessment, or to record student marks. Failure to involve everyone, as appropriate, in the team can lead to confusion and misunderstanding of course requirements; poor alignment of teaching and assessment approaches; and a lack of confidence in the course from both staff and students. When it comes to teaching beyond the classroom, then more people are often involved than we might imagine. This is one welcome benefit of the shift going on in higher education across the world towards a preparation for employment. In Case study 6.4, Davies and Dennis recognise that the student experience in a workplace setting depends on a whole host of people. Collective practice doesn't just depend on those with most immediate control of teaching. There can be significant value in working collectively with all those who have a stake.

Case study 6.4
ENGAGING THE ENTIRE WORK COMMUNITY

Nancy Davies and Caitriona Dennis, Leeds Institute of
Teaching Excellence, University of Leeds

A busy hospital ward or clinic is the setting for the vast majority of medical teaching. This is a challenging, pressurised environment where educational training is under-resourced and consequential to the primary nature of the work. In order to learn, medical students look to the whole healthcare team and patients and carers, i.e., universal faculty, for opportunities to increase their knowledge and enhance skills and professionalism. Consequently, in any given placement, students may encounter several staff who provide the role of 'tutor'. As trainers of medical education, we recognise that this poses a challenge as teaching skills are not enforced outside of the university resulting in workplace 'tutors' providing a variable experience for the students.

On placement, a healthcare professional maybe asked by the student to provide constructive feedback on their competency in a particular clinical scenario. From the University's perspective, we recognise this as an area when an interaction is required between university and placement in order not only to enhance and enrich not only skills in educational practice but also to promote a wider understanding of learning goals and the undergraduate curriculum in general.

TiMEToTeach is an educational outreach initiative providing support in the form of Continuing Professional Development (CPD) sessions. It acts as a bridge between academic and professional learning environments to provide educational support and basic teaching skills not just to the main staff supporting students on placement but the whole 'work community' they will interact with. Goodie bags are given as part of sessions to say thank-you to the Universal Faculty for supporting our students. They contain branded freebies such as pens and lanyards which help students identify those who are keen to teach. Also included are postcards with easy to digest facts about key teaching innovations which can be read and passed on to colleagues.

In our TiMEToTeach sessions we promote scholarly dialogue emphasising good practice and recognising those who have impacted our students' education. One particular session we were able to thank the whole placement staff including receptionists for providing excellent student experience as evidenced through positive placement feedback from students. As a result the staff were inspired to request further teaching skills training through university-based CPD events.

A consequence of the TiMEToTeach promotion, through feedback from staff, students and patients, is that we have been able to educate and enthuse universal Faculty in helping to shape medical education and enhance the student experience in placements. More than this it is an opportunity to create an educational community of practice out in the wider working world. To enable all placement people to benefit from the student relationship (however brief) by helping them to understand innovations in their area and of 'how things work' for the students.

It brings the University outside the establishment walls and truly integrates it with the working world for a more holistic experience for students, placement staff and the wider public. It is an enactment of the citizenship behaviour we hope to foster in our students.

CONCLUSIONS

In some ways the approach to developing your teaching that we have advocated in this chapter holds out the greatest possibilities for enhancing teaching amongst all of the possibilities covered in this book. Colleagues, though, don't always respond when they are asked to or actually deliver on what they promise. We are all aware of the increasing pressures on staff workloads and expectations in higher education. The pressure of emails has loomed large for both of us even as we set about writing this book. Patience is needed when working with colleagues, as is a good dose of self-efficacy. Think about what it is that might bring you, your colleagues, your students and others together. Take the time to find out about the interests and priorities of others, and then carry forward new initiatives together.

REFERENCES

Castells, M. (2010). *The Rise of the Network Society*. Chichester: Wiley-Blackwell.

Gibbs, G., Knapper, C. & Piccinin, S. (2008). Disciplinary and contextually appropriate approaches to leadership of teaching in research-intensive academic departments in higher education. *Higher Education Quarterly*, 62(4), 416–36.

Gustavsen, B. (2001). Theory and practice: The mediating discourse. In P. Reason & H. Bradbury, *Handbook of Action Research: The Concise Paperback Edition* (pp. 17–26). Thousand Oaks, CA: SAGE.

Jessop, T., El-Hakim, Y. & Gibbs, G. (2011). The TESTA project: research inspiring change. *Educational Developments*, 12(4), 12–16.

Jessop, T. & Tomas, C. (2017). The implications of programme assessment patterns for student learning. *Assessment & Evaluation in Higher Education*, 42(6), 990–9.

Kahn, P. E. (2014). Theorising student engagement in higher education. *British Educational Research Journal*, 40(6), 1005 – 18.

Kahn, P. E. & Baume, D. (2003). *A Guide to Staff and Educational Development* (1st edition). Abingdon: Routledge.

Laidlaw, D. (2003). Collaborative classroom teaching of art/computation/science. *The Teaching Exchange*, 7(2).

Richardson, M., Abraham, C. & Bond, R. (2012). Psychological correlates of university students' academic performance: A systematic review and meta-analysis. *Psychological Bulletin*, 138(2), 353.

Salmon, G., Ross, B., Pechenkina, E. & Chase, A.-M. (2015). The space for social media in structured online learning. *Research in Learning Technology*, 23.

Schwarzer, R. (2014). *Self-efficacy: Thought Control of Action*. New York: Taylor & Francis.

FURTHER READING

Kenway, J., Epstein, D. & Boden, R. (2005). *Building Networks*. London: SAGE.
Walsh, L. & Kahn, P. E. (2010). *Collaborative Working in Higher Education: The Social Academy*. London: Routledge.

Chapter 7

Connecting to drivers

> . . . what drives us to change? Knowledge is increasing rapidly, learners have become more diverse, demand for higher education has increased, and technology continually offers new opportunities. Pedagogies must also adjust. We have become a global community of teachers and learners as we share what we know and benefit from what others share.
> (Maureen Andrade, Utah Valley University)

INTRODUCTION

It has become a truism that change is the new constant. And while this may be acknowledged, it does not mean that it has become a normalised concept within our practice. We can still react badly to the idea of change, and even when it looks to be opening doors and creating new opportunities, it may still appear to us to be threatening, frightening or at the very least, disconcerting and troublesome. The way in which we view change can, however, depend on the driver behind it. As Andrade indicates above in the opening quote to this chapter, drivers can take many forms including legislative, environmental and technological; or may have their origins in the student body or as a result of our own personal reflections.

Understanding change is the first step to feeling more in control of its effects. Behind every change is an impetus or catalyst. These are the drivers with which we must engage in order to be able to understand and effect meaningful change; and not to be simply swept up in its path. How can we learn to look more positively on drivers for change within our professional context? And to harness these drivers for the benefit of ourselves and our students? Drivers can provide opportunities as well as challenges – so how might we utilise them to develop our teaching?

TABLE 7.1 High impact practices (Bass, 2012: 26)

First-year seminars and experiences	Common intellectual experiences	Learning communities	Writing-intensive courses	Collaborative assignments and projects
Undergraduate research	Diversity/global learning (study abroad)	Service learning, community-based learning	Internships	Capstone courses and projects

Many drivers can be helpful and supportive of practice development as opposed to presenting a challenge or a threat. This can be seen through this example of student feedback as a driver for change on an international scale that originated with the National Survey of Student Engagement (NSSE) in the US. Feedback from the NSSE identified a number of teaching approaches that demonstrated a correlation with what were defined as 'meaningful learning gains' (Kuh, 2008) and high retention and progression rates. This list has become known as 'high impact practices' and has had a significant impact on the sector.

Table 7.1 represents an example of a high level and influential, evidence-based and student-centred impetus for change within practice – everything that we would want to see in an effective driver. It is unlikely that you would want (or indeed be able!) to adopt all of these approaches within your curriculum but they provide leverage and justification for change. This chapter looks at a range of current drivers in higher education and discusses ways in which you might connect and engage with them, whether they pose challenges or provide opportunities, in order to develop your teaching.

WORKING WITH DRIVERS

Your perspective on drivers will depend on your relationship to them. In some situations you may feel or find yourself to be on the periphery of a driver or catalyst for change, such as an institutional learning and teaching strategy. You may find yourself caught up in the change without feeling that you have any agency to influence its direction. In order to help you focus on developing your teaching, however, you need to

CONNECTING TO DRIVERS

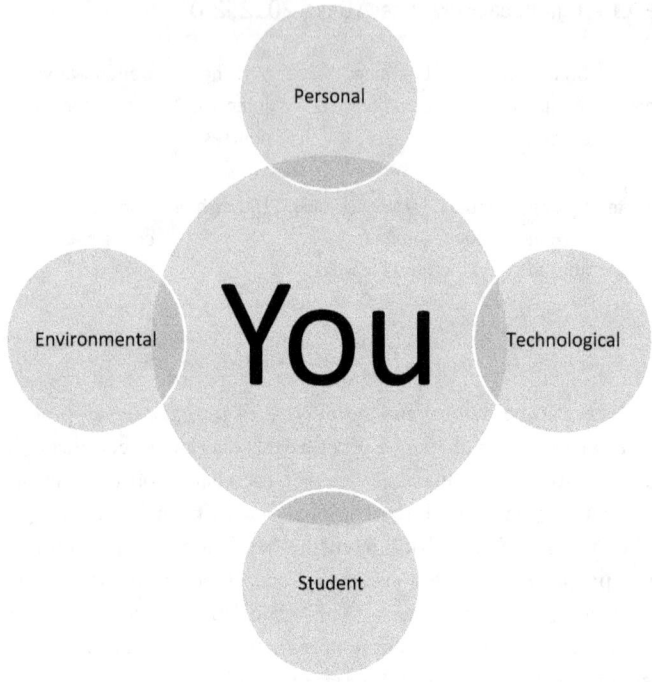

FIGURE 7.1 Drivers that impact practice

put yourself at the centre of the drivers that you feel are impacting your practice, as demonstrated in Figure 7.1. This will give you a different perspective on the situation and greater insight into how you can deal with their influence.

The drivers that you encounter will be numerous and varied but we've identified four here to get you thinking: environmental, student, personal and technological. We've selected these examples as they relate to other aspects of practice that we discuss across the book including the teaching landscape, our working relationship with our students, our own personal and professional development, and the wider sector-level impetuses for change, using the example here of technological and digital change.

Environmental drivers

Environmental drivers can be some of the most challenging to control; but can also present numerous opportunities to reflect on our teaching.

They can include those that impact us at a macro level, including legislative and sector-wide influences such as an increasing move to measure everything in higher education or the introduction of mandatory 'training' – whether that be for teaching or wrestling with data protection issues or cyber-security. The introduction of new frameworks to support learning and teaching, or researcher development, can feel like impositions rather than useful developments, leaving us feeling resentful rather than enthused. Expectations and responses to changes at the level of the wider global environment therefore directly influence our local experience. We can feel disconnected from these effects, however, if we feel we have had no say in their development and perhaps aggrieved at the demands they make on our time or requirements to change our practice – even if we can appreciate their importance. We literally feel 'put upon'; and we don't like it!

Drivers can also affect us at the micro level, through influences on our day-to-day teaching practice, such as a new marking and grading scale or timetable changes. Let's look at a specific example. If you are asked to run a module in a steeply raked lecture theatre does that mean you have to give a formal lecture – for every class? If you are allocated a long, flat teaching room with poor acoustics and groups of tables does this mean that you are restricted to small group work – for every class? Does a 9 a.m., Monday morning – or 4 p.m., Friday afternoon – teaching slot on your timetable instill a feeling of dread in you (and your students!)? The answer to each of these questions should be no. Rather than feeling constrained or inhibited in our practice by these developments we should look at the opportunities they provide to think differently about our practice. Returning to the timetabled lecture slot, we don't need to fall back on traditional didactic teaching approaches as active learning is quite possible in any kind of environment; even a lecture theatre.

- Pair students up to discuss questions.
- Encourage students to come into your space by asking them to scribe on the whiteboard.
- Move into their space by walking up the side of the lecture theatre when they're discussing questions.
- Mix up the tutor-student environments in the lecture theatre and see the class dynamics change!

Similarly, in a small group teaching environment, don't be afraid to move the furniture in order to realise the environment that you want to achieve. Even better, get the students to move the furniture for you as a 'warm up' activity – and to put it back again! If you anticipate a timetabled teaching slot will be challenging for you and your students, whether in terms of motivation, engagement or the logistics of travel or perhaps childcare responsibilities, think about what changes you might make to the structure of your teaching session to ameliorate the effects. Is it possible to have a slightly later start and to provide any elements of the session that you feel may be compromised as result through additional online content? Might some of the classes be replaced by a podcast or vodcast? In a two-hour class could one of the hours take on a flipped classroom approach, where students review online material or reading in advance of using the remaining in-class hour for intensive discussion or debate or practical exercises?

Review point 7.1
IDENTIFYING YOUR DRIVERS

- What other drivers can you identify within your department or school?
- Are they local, with relatively limited impact, or are they at sector level with widespread impact and importance?
- Do they drive you to change your practice in ways that you can manage? If yes, how can you leverage benefit for your teaching from these changes?
- If not, what strategies can you put in place or networks on which you can draw to ameliorate or manage the change?

Student drivers

In Chapter 4 we looked at partnership working with our students and undoubtedly one of the most important drivers comes from your students where your role is as an intermediary in the change process, e.g. student feedback as an impetus for change. Student feedback can be gathered in a number of ways, both formal and informal, including face-to-face discussions, traditional paper-based feedback questionnaires or increasingly through online surveys. While some of these will be at module level others will be large-scale sector-wide surveys, such as the National Student Survey (NSS) and the International Student Barometer (ISB) in the UK and the National Survey of Student Engagement (NSSE) in the US, where there is significant pressure on students and staff to ensure that the surveys are completed as international ranking, league tables, benchmarking and associated reputational loss or gain are dependent on good returns.

Implementing any approach to gathering feedback is associated with a number of challenges; the process can become routine and in a data-driven environment with a central focus on capturing the 'student voice', learners are in real danger of being over-surveyed, resulting in questionnaire fatigue and correspondingly poor or banal responses. You may find yourself having to use a standard institutional or departmental questionnaire for some of your teaching but don't let this stop you also using your own methods to elicit the feedback that you need to develop your practice – although this doesn't mean providing every student with two feedback forms! Consider other approaches with more personalised and interactive formats, such as staff – student committees and focus groups. Body language, vocal tone and facial expressions often speak more loudly than the written word! Face-to-face contact also means, of course, that you can clarify issues and ask students to expand on particular responses, resulting in a much richer, deeper and more valuable form of feedback.

Any kind of approach to gathering feedback in and of itself raises a raft of common concerns:

- Students only tell you what they think you want to hear.
- Students only use feedback forms as an opportunity to complain.
- The kinds of students who give fulsome replies aren't representative.

And this is probably only scraping the surface of lecturers' complaints and concerns, however, feedback questionnaires often provide students with little incentive to complete them. Questions such as 'Was I an effective teacher?' or 'How well did I structure the classes?' mean little to students who may never cross your path again. In order to encourage genuine and useful responses from our students we need to focus on their learning, what *they* have gained from the classes. Asking students to rate your teaching is actually asking them to carry out a difficult task for which they have little prior experience and often no wider context within which to situate that experience. As we've seen throughout the book, and will discuss in more detail in Chapter 10, it is exceedingly difficult for experienced colleagues to decide on what constitutes excellence in teaching, let alone students.

The important things to remember when asking our students for feedback include the following.

- Ask them about their *learning* rather than your *teaching*. We need to ask the questions that can help us to find out more about how well our students are learning as a result of our teaching, not just how entertaining or enjoyable our teaching may be. This is the kind of feedback that can genuinely help us to develop our practice. The focus of our two teacher-centred questions above therefore becomes 'Were you able to learn effectively in this class?' and 'What made that learning possible for you?'
- Ask about what you want to know but also ensure that it is within your power to make changes in these areas e.g. don't ask students if they would prefer a larger, brighter, warmer or cooler teaching room if it is not possible to provide one. Think carefully not only about what you want to ask but how you want to ask it. Pose questions that are concise, clear and to the point; address only one issue in each question in order to avoid confusion, or receiving an answer to only half a question.
- Don't wait until the end of the year, when your current students have moved on, before you make changes. Adopt a 'you said, we did' approach – ask them before the end of the module or course of study, as well as at the end, so that they can benefit from any changes made and then let them know that you've done it. You could use a physical feedback board for this if you have a dedicated course area, wall space or teaching room. Or an online equivalent such as Padlet. Or an in-class voting tool using smartphones. Alternatively – and you will need to take this approach if your students are distance learners – use an area on your course VLE or blog, etc.

In this case study Helen Robson, from the Institute of Social Work and Applied Social Studies at the University of Staffordshire, demonstrates how she uses a variety of formal and informal methods, including written feedback and observation of student behaviour and reactions, in order to inform the development of her teaching practice. Note also how Helen actively employs the strategies of reflecting 'in' and 'on' practice, as discussed in Chapter 5, in order to inform her teaching.

Case study 7.1
USING STUDENT FEEDBACK TO INFORM FUTURE PRACTICE

Helen Robson, University of Staffordshire

Students will not always say what they liked or disliked about a session or course without prompting; sometimes the only way a teacher may know about the effectiveness of his or her teaching is when the students leave the course – i.e. 'vote with their feet'! I find one of the most effective and immediate ways of improving teaching is to actively look for information from students. Even without being proactive in seeking feedback, it is difficult not to be aware of student behaviour in class (for example, looking puzzled or bored, or talking amongst themselves).

Apart from the formal evaluation procedures required by the University, when I am teaching I look for three main criteria by which to judge my practice: the students' level of interest in the subject, their level of understanding of the subject, and their response to the teaching method. I can gauge their level of interest in the subject by being aware of their body language and by how many and what sort of questions they ask. I can judge the level of understanding of the subject by both the types of questions asked, and the answers provided to my questions. Evaluating my choice of teaching method can be done by noting students' willingness to participate and through the outcomes of assessment.

I then use this information to review and reflect on my teaching in two ways: first, I can adjust my lesson plan during a teaching session in an immediate response to student feedback. This method of thinking on my feet, described by Donald Schön as 'reflection-in-action', means that if it is evident that the students have not understood the material I've just delivered, I think about spending more time on the topic, or explaining it in a different way, before moving on. Second, it involves looking back on a session, or carrying out 'reflection-on-action', and in light of the experience, amending it for next time, or altering the next session. This would happen if, for example, student feedback suggested that there was not enough interaction, or my presentation had been unclear or uninteresting. By regularly reviewing my practice in this way, and using student feedback to inform and support my development, I feel I am continually improving my teaching.

Once you have obtained feedback on your teaching, what next? Consider how you will respond to the feedback. What changes might you make in light of the comments? How can you build on the positive areas? How will you communicate those changes to your students? Learning from student feedback can help to inform your practice in a number of ways including supporting you in developing a better understanding of how students learn; appreciating what works and what doesn't in terms of your teaching practice; 'road testing' new teaching approaches; responding effectively to student concerns or anxieties; and validating your current approach to practice. Integrate the process of gathering feedback within your teaching; don't just employ it as a bolt-on or after-thought. At the planning stages of a new course or lecture series, think carefully about what kind of feedback mechanisms would be most appropriate and how you will implement them.

Perhaps the students' response is not quite what you had anticipated. Dealing with criticism can be difficult but always review student feedback objectively and get a colleague to help you in order to carry out this process more effectively. In a group of 99 per cent positive feedback it is that 1 per cent that will niggle away at you. Put it into perspective. Does that student raise a valid issue? Is it a matter that might be of concern to a wider group? Is the student just making 'a point'? Alternatively, you might want to reflect on the 99 per cent. Is such a positive response an accurate reflection of the student learning experience in your classes? Have you asked the right questions – are they sufficiently probing, clear and targeted in order to help you find out what you want to know? Think about other feedback mechanisms you may use in future.

Personal drivers

Other drivers for change can come from your personal reflections on your own practice, career aspirations and the avenues you choose to explore, whether that be project funding or a promoted post or a complete change of focus. This can be through personal scholarship or an exploration of your own values, teaching philosophy and actual teaching experience. In the following case study, Bethan Wood, from the School of Interdisciplinary Studies, University of Glasgow (Dumfries), reflects on how her experiences of teaching in the secondary or senior school sector was a driver for her to change her practice as a university teacher.

 **Case study 7.2**
IT WORKED!

Bethan Wood, University of Glasgow (Dumfries)

Prior to becoming a teaching academic I taught Scottish secondary pupils science and biology for nine years; undeniably, they are the best critics of your teaching. Not for them the subtleties of surreptitiously looking at the phone under the table, or sending electronic notes to peers. They will let you know quite explicitly when they don't understand something or that they are bored — orally or behaviourally, it doesn't matter to them! Teaching at this level was therefore one of the best preparations I could have had for my university career as it developed the teaching and learning skills I have come to utilise in my academic teaching today. It taught me what works (teaching with activities), what doesn't (just lecturing), what stimulates (practical activities – especially outside if practicable), what bores (constant talking at them), and when to have a break (body language).

When I arrived at university I immediately started teaching a level 3 course and quite frankly my first lecture was a bit of disaster. The content was not sufficient for the period allocated and I had 30 minutes at the end to fill. I therefore sat down and started asking the students about themselves. I also told them a little about myself (background and career) and discussed how they would feel if instead of me talking through a PowerPoint presentation, I supplemented our 'lecture' time with various activities. This appeared to be something that few other lecturers did at that time, but we agreed to try it for the rest of the semester and that they would feed back to me on what worked and what didn't.

The next week I started with small group discussions. This involved them discussing a point on the slide with others near them and then feeding back to the whole group. For me, the time passed very quickly indicating that I was personally engaged with what we were all doing. At the end of the session I asked them how they felt the session had gone and the feedback was positive; all stating that they understood more of the content as a result of the discussions and that the time had passed quickly.

Fifteen years on, I still do not give a traditional 'lecture'. I include a variety of activities throughout my allocated periods which can include: small calculation exercises, analysis of graphs or information to feed back to the whole group, the original small discussion groups, small debates, and short videos with discussion at the end. Having these activities interspersed provide breather points – for both my students and me. Student evaluations over the years have proved to me that this style of academic teaching does work; with students feeding back that they enjoyed the activities and the course overall. As a small campus we do have the benefit of small to medium sized classes, however, I've also used this style with a larger class at the main campus – and it worked!

Personal drivers can also come through developing a more reflexive approach to your practice. Reflexivity can be a slippery concept but is articulated well here by Manwaring (2017: 172) who uses a mirror analogy to capture both the essence and practical application of the idea: '. . . a concave mirror reflecting the past, a microscope for self-analysis, a periscope for horizon scanning, and a convex mirror beaming forward'.

Essentially, reflexivity can be viewed as a: 'metacognitive approach encompassing many attributes such as critical thinking, emotional intelligence and professionalism . . . [helping] professionals deal with unpredictable situations and manage change sensitively' (Manwaring, 2017: 174). Reflexivity is an extension of the reflective process that we looked at in Chapter 5. It allows for a more student and learning focused perspective on practice, moving personal reflection and action for change into the domain of the wider learning environment and experience. It is a practice that draws on the benefit of the collective rather than the individual – something we looked at in Chapter 6 – where '[d]ialogue and discussion . . . allow greater understanding of what has happened and the reasons behind behavior and the role of the learner' (ibid.: 178). Reflexivity as a driver can therefore be highly beneficial for your practice and can involve you in exploring a number of approaches to expand your role as a teaching professional. These might include:

- investigating your practice through an action research or appreciative inquiry approach
- taking part in an action learning set
- re-evaluating your personal philosophy of teaching in light of discussions with colleagues from different disciplinary backgrounds who teach in different ways
- (really) listening to the experiences of a wide variety of students and triangulating their views with your own perspectives to generate new learning

- preparing an application for professional recognition through Advance HE or your discipline-based professional body.

Working with these ideas can impact the other personal drivers in your life, such as career aspirations, in potentially unexpected ways. While there is an expectation that we may follow a path of progress through promotion and advancement, this linear approach can be narrow and restrictive; and may end up in a bottleneck. Use the approaches identified above to see what other options may be available to you. We'll revisit this topic and this particular driver again in Chapter 11.

Technological drivers

One of the most commonly acknowledged drivers for change in our teaching practice is technology. Digital technologies and online learning have become ubiquitous in the higher education landscape and yet in some ways they are still viewed as new or emerging approaches to teaching and learning. E-learning and e-assessment have become mainstreamed and yet we may continue to have distinct e-learning policies and perhaps e-learning committees or awards for online teaching. Digital approaches to learning therefore continue to be differentiated from 'traditional' approaches, largely as a result of the relentless driver that they provide. Digital technologies continue to develop at a very fast rate of change so are always headline news. 'Like dog years, technology years go by faster than human years. In other words, the velocity of change is increasing' (LeBlanc, 2018: 54).

Drivers may not necessarily result in change in the ways in which it was anticipated, particularly in relation to technology. Even though some of the early promise of online approaches has failed to materialise as anticipated (think about virtual worlds, for example), as they are constantly replaced by new approaches the momentum of expectation is therefore sustained. As the technological 'tail' can tend to wag the pedagogical 'dog', this means that technology can tend to forefront teaching activity, providing it with a higher and distinctive profile. You may be excited by technology in your teaching or be quite accepting of it as the norm in your practice. Despite its social ubiquity, however, not every student is comfortable with digital technologies in a learning environment. Not every student has, chooses to have − or indeed should be expected to have − a smartphone. Not every student has access to a charged and functioning tablet or laptop to use in every class − or for out of class study. And while today's younger students may have grown up digital, that doesn't mean that they want to engage with the tools in which their day-to-day social lives are immersed, for the purposes of academic study. We therefore continue to inhabit a middle ground between traditional and fully digital teaching that sees some elements of morphing and overlap but which resists full acculturation. The drivers to encourage us to do so are, nonetheless, relentless.

Think about the technological drivers that currently impact your teaching. Some of these will be high level. *Confronting the Challenges of Participatory Culture* (Jenkins, Clinton, Purushotma, Robison & Weigel, n.d.) saw the developing online or 'participatory cultures' such as Wikipedia, blogs and online communities as drivers for change to the formal curriculum-based approach to student learning. Meanwhile, the Association of American Colleges and Universities' *Greater Expectations* report (2002) identified the need for change in this area in response to the growing participation rate in the US higher education system. There may be other local reports and surveys in your own institution that flag up anticipated directions of travel in the digital environment. These will be reflected in the approaches or tools you are required to use, perhaps your institutional VLE and increasingly online assessment submission through academic integrity checking software; while others may be optional, such as in-class polling or voting tools or discussion boards and blogs. You'll probably use some of the tools extensively only with your colleagues, email for example, and have to use other approaches to reach your students. And then there will be tools that you choose to use because of your own personal or disciplinary interest, and similarly those that your students expect you to use, such as mainstream social media platforms.

Review point 7.2
WORKING WITH YOUR DIGITAL DRIVERS

- What digital tools do you choose to use in your teaching? Why is this?
- Are your choices driven more from your personal interest – or student demand?
- What digital tools do you have to use? Why is this?
- What tools would you like to use in the future?
- What's driving your decisions?

IDENTIFYING DRIVERS FOR POSITIVE CHANGE

Drivers are therefore multifarious; and potentially never-ending! Where should you put your energies? How can you evaluate the relative importance of different drivers? Might it make a difference to introduce a change supported by a driver, rather than pursuing a change without one, but that is still important to you – and your students. Recognised drivers can provide vehicles on which to 'piggy-back' your ideas and can smooth the political road and iron out resourcing difficulties, to some extent. Research projects which attract small pots of seed corn funding can be a good way to start.

You need to identify strategies to manage your approach to drivers, which must be as proactive as possible, in order to keep abreast of new drivers, particularly in the fast-moving field of technological change. Horizon scanning is an important aspect of this approach. There are several well established 'go to' resources for this including the *Times Higher Education Supplement* (THES) and in the UK, WonkHE, the self-proclaimed 'home of higher education wonks'. There are also annually produced resources such as the Open University Innovating Pedagogy reports and, with a greater focus on technologies to support teaching and learning, the New Media Consortium (NMC) Horizon reports, produced by EDUCAUSE. Bodies such as Advance HE, the Carnegie Foundation for the Advancement of Teaching, and the Higher Education Research and Development Society of Australasia (HERDSA) also focus on current topics and produce a range of resources. So far, so good. Lots of information, on a regular basis; but how can you manage the volume and discriminate between what you want to read, need to read and should be reading?

- You may want to focus on an area of particular interest to you and your students, but you also need to be mindful of institutional priorities and the direction of travel within your disciplinary area.
- There are also drivers that impact our teaching on a global level, such as digital capabilities, that are impossible to avoid and therefore necessary to engage with.
- Beware of fads. There are many blind alleys or slow burners that need to be either avoided or handled with caution, particularly within an area such as digital technologies. Look for reliable guidance. The annual NMC Horizon Reports, for example, provide useful indicators on the short, mid and long-term likelihood of adoption of particular technologies and

time-to-adoption estimates for technological developments over the next one to five years.

Also keep in regular contact with the published literature in your field and wider educational drivers.

Review point 7.3
TAKING STOCK OF YOUR POTENTIAL DRIVERS

- What fora exist in your department to explore drivers for change in a positive way?
- How might you work with colleagues to leverage change through local drivers?

CONCLUSIONS

Identifying drivers, engaging with drivers and even creating drivers ourselves are therefore important aspects of professional practice. Drivers affect what resources might be likely to exist or whether you can secure funding for a project. They can influence our career direction and the ways in which we teach. Being at least aware, if not in actual control of drivers, is an important part of managing their potential impact without feeling overwhelmed. Horizon scanning and anticipating change are therefore important aspects of professional practice, allowing drivers to provide an ideal chance to take the opportunity to 'disrupt' our normal practice and to reconsider and reflect upon our teaching, rather than viewing them as harbingers of fear or concern. Look at ways in which current drivers can be employed to leverage change and development within your teaching. Being aware and taking control are the first steps to empowerment and enhancement of practice.

 REFERENCES

Association of American Colleges and Universities (2002). *Greater Expectations: A New Vision for Learning as a Nation Goes to College*. Washington. [Online, accessed 16 September, 2018].

Bass, R. (2012). Disrupting ourselves: The problem of learning in higher education. *EDUCAUSE Review*, 47(2) (March/April). https://er.educause.edu/articles/2012/3/disrupting-ourselves-the-problem-of-learning-in-higher-education [Online, accessed 16 September, 2018].

EDUCAUSE (and the NMC Horizon reports). www.educause.edu [Online, accessed 16 September, 2018].

HERDSA. www.herdsa.org.au [Online, accessed 16 September, 2018].

Institute of Educational Technology Innovating Pedagogy Reports. Open University, https://iet.open.ac.uk/innovating-pedagogy [Online, accessed 16 September, 2018].

Jenkins, H., Clinton, K., Purushotma, R. Robison, A. & Weigel, M. (n.d). *Confronting the Challenges of Participatory Culture: Media Education for the 21st Century*. Chicago: The MacArthur Foundation.

Kuh, G. (2008). *High-Impact Educational Practices: What They Are, Who Has Access to Them, and Why They Matter*. AAC&U.

LeBlanc, P. (2018). Reading Signals from the Future: EDUCAUSE in 2038. *EDUCAUSE Review* 53, no. 4 (July/August). https://er.educause.edu/articles/2018/7/reading-signals-from-the-future-educause-in-2038 [Online, accessed 16 September, 2018].

Manwaring, G. (2017). The reflexive graduate. In C. Normand & L. Anderson (eds.), *Graduate Attributes in Higher Education. Attitudes on attributes from across the disciplines*. Abingdon/New York: Routledge.

Times Higher Education (THES). www.timeshighereducation.com [Online, accessed 16 September, 2018].

WonkHE: policy, people and politics. www.wonkhe.com [Online, accessed 16 September, 2018].

Chapter 8
Researching your own practice

INTRODUCTION: MAKING A DIFFERENCE

Which discipline do you think is the most prestigious, the one whose research you consider to be regarded most highly by others? Medical researchers, certainly, seem to attract the largest salaries in universities. If citation reports are anything to go by, then, the biosciences, materials science, immunology, nanotechnology, economics and finance might all try to lay claim to the mantle of most-highly-regarded-discipline. There is certainly some scepticism, though, around the value of educational research. Education is unlikely to figure all that highly in your own pecking order of disciplines in the university. Given this, why would you invest significant time and energy in mastering research into your own practice?

Nonetheless, there is an array of evidence that educational research can make a significant difference to how well students learn and to the quality of teaching in universities. One could go on almost endlessly with study after study, but the following gives a taste of some of overall perspectives:

- An extensive research agenda in the USA has identified a set of educational practices that have been linked to high levels of student engagement and retention (Kuh and Schneider, 2008). These include courses that emphasise the process of writing, collaborative assignments and projects, service learning and work placements. (See also Chapter 7 on connecting to drivers.)
- Richardson, Abraham and Bond (2012) found a particularly close connection between the self-efficacy of students and academic performance (as noted in Chapter 6).
- The second order meta-anlaysis by Tamim, Bernard, Borokhovski, Abrami and Schmid (2011) identified a significant (if

modest) impact of educational innovations on student achievement where technology was employed rather than traditional instruction. Learning technology covers a wide range of interventions, of course, but they noted that its impact was greater where technology was used to support instruction rather than to provide it.
- Gurin, Dey, Hurtado, and Gurin (2002) demonstrated the value of a diverse student body to intercultural understanding.

You can certainly shape your own practice in light of research that has been carried out by others, as we saw in Chapter 2. Some studies have specifically suggested, though, that the impact of educational research can be particularly significant where practitioners themselves are involved in the research. Hamilton and Appleby (2009) argued that such research has identified benefits such as improvement in practice, challenges to policy, and knowledge that is directly relevant to practice. This contrasts with the areas listed above as potentially vying for the mantle of the most prestigious discipline. These former areas of research are characterised by a detached stance towards the object of the research. Nonetheless, it is quite reasonable to defend insider research: research that is undertaken on matters that relate to an organisation by full members of that organisation. And taking it down to the granular level, insider research includes research undertaken by you on your own area of practice. Brannick and Coghlan (2007) found no inherent reasons why being a native should be a problem when researching, despite some commentators claiming otherwise. The challenges that come from already possessing knowledge about life within an organisation, for instance, are not insurmountable within any of the main research traditions of educational research. There is a potential for conflict between one's role within the organisation and one's role as a researcher, but, equally, insider status can be of assistance in galvanising a groundswell for change.

Given the huge influence that the discipline, institution, department, student body, staff body and other locally determined factors all play on learning, research that is tailored to your own context and needs has significant scope to make a difference. Research into your own practice can also be expected to support your own commitment as a teacher, especially when your career is focused on teaching and scholarship. The original model of scholarship developed by Boyer (1990), indeed, proposed different forms of scholarship that were focused on discovery (i.e. research), integration, application and teaching. Trigwell and Shale (2004) described a scholarship of teaching with three temporal components: *awareness* of conceptions of practice, knowledge itself, and development processes; the *ability* to carry out developments that involve investigation, reflection, collaboration and learning; and a readiness to deliver *outcomes* that move teaching in the discipline forward, provide the developer with satisfaction, and leave artefacts behind (see also Ashwin and Trigwell, 2004). Investigation is a central element in achieving scholarship of this depth, offering a rich vein of interactions with knowledge, practice, students and colleagues. A scholarly approach to teaching can stand alongside our subject research as an activity in which we can invest ourselves.

It is certainly the case that contracts of employment that are focused on teaching and scholarship rather than on teaching and research are now increasingly common. Nonetheless, the recognition and reward systems that operate within higher education do generally contain an expectation that staff with careers focused on the scholarship of teaching will engage in publication. One of the most obvious ways to leave artefacts behind is to publish. You might take a look at the way that publication manifests itself in the promotion criteria operating in this area in your own institution. Educational research can provide a highly effective means to supporting a career that is focused on teaching.

What are the ways, then, of getting into research that is relevant to your own practice as an educator? In the rest of this chapter we will look at some routes into researching your own practice. Evaluation provides an immediate entry point – this is typically expected of most staff carrying responsibility for teaching in universities. It may be possible to take advantage of your own disciplinary expertise, given that education can be researched from a range of positions. Nonetheless, undertaking an advanced qualification in education could still make a significant difference, as would conducting research alongside others.

MAKING A START WITH EVALUATION

A key driver behind much educational research is to improve teaching and learning. A fundamental question for research is then to ask how well current provision is working: evaluation. In the case study that follows, Dave Roberts indicates how he was dissatisfied when he had to sit through text-dominated slides during conferences. Only then did he realise that his own teaching was much the same. Taking this realisation seriously led to innovations with high quality digital images. He then kept on asking his students what they thought of his changes and innovations. That is, he began with a straightforward evaluation of his innovations.

Case study 8.1
DEATH BY POWERPOINT

Dave Roberts, School of Business and Economics, Loughborough University

My greatest learning about my own teaching came from being on the receiving end of it. It came as a shock to realise how disengaged I was with conference presentations dominated by text-filled slides. It came as a bigger shock to realise that I was doing the same thing to my students. I was getting a taste of my own medicine. I asked them. They nodded. I said I'd do better.

I found widespread condemnation of the orthodox lecture method itself that needs no rehearsal here. But I also found four things that inspired me. The first was creative advertising. I was enthralled by the ways that one image and a few words could tell a complex story. The second was the rise of the digital image. Billions are uploaded annually, and there are billions more to come. The third was the presentation 'guru' (don't stop reading). The ones I'm thinking of, like Nancy Duarte and Guy Kawasaki, shared the same concerns I had: how could I better engage an audience? They were telling me to reduce text and use imagery and their demos were engaging. They used the same software I did but differently, so it became increasingly clear this was about *how* we used PowerPoint (or Prezi, Keynote and so on); you wouldn't blame Word for a bad article and we shouldn't blame PowerPoint for a bad lecture. These three coalesced around the fourth, Multimedia Learning, or MML. MML posits, on the back of half a century of scholarship and millennia of common knowledge, that we learn better with images and words than words alone, because sighted people are 'dual processors' of knowledge: we have audio-textual and visual channels. The ad wo/men, the gurus and the scholars agree: more equitable use of text and imagery in slides reduces the load on working memory and improves engagement accordingly.

I started using images and dispersing text across slides and in 'notes view'. I asked my students what they thought. They nodded again. Then some wrote to me in appreciation. I transformed all my lectures and began a separate three-year longitudinal control group experiment. Students were subject and object of the research; I created a web tool to encourage their participation and began testing for engagement and active learning characteristics, identified from the relevant scholarly literature. The results were worth sharing. I could apply the research to the teaching of subjects in my own field and published in the journals' teaching and learning sections of my disciplinary area. In addition, because the MML approach is about cognition not content, it's theoretically applicable to all disciplines, so I published them in pedagogical journals as well. I presented (and continue to present) at conferences and other outlets in the UK and USA, and I started to write blogs on 'how to' for anyone interested, followed by the creation of a Community of Practice and a small consultancy. By sharing the process this way, I got great feedback that helped me start closing some of the holes in the approach, which I could feed back into my own teaching. It was another circle of learning, beginning with discomfort, continuing with introspection and reflection, growing to development and evaluation and then student and peer-review. I feel better about my teaching: I'm happier in my work, and my students are too, if their annual feedback is anything to go by. I wish it had happened sooner; I hope it happens again.

Feedback from students does provide a starting point for evaluation, but it has its limitations. After all, it isn't always that easy to tell whether your teaching or your students' learning has improved – some students may now be learning more effectively than others. Many developments are indeed limited to the immediate context in which they are carried out. Without a more systematic understanding of why something has worked, it is difficult to transfer lessons to other contexts. If excellence is to be transferred from one person to another, or from one department to another (as we shall explore further in the chapter on teaching excellence), then it is essential to understand why innovations are effective.

More rigorous evaluation certainly requires you to adopt a well thought out methodology, perhaps along the lines of Saunders (2000). You will usually need to go beyond evaluation that just looks at grades and student feedback, even if these are important nonetheless, drawing on data from a variety of sources to improve the trustworthiness of your findings through what is termed 'triangulation'. Yet such evaluation is essential if the development is to serve your practice more widely, and indeed be of much use to colleagues. Ashwin and Trigwell (2004), for instance, made a distinction between investigations that are designed to produce knowledge of relevance to oneself and local knowledge that is of relevance to one's colleagues.

Review point 8.1
GOING FOR IT

- Think of an innovation that you think worked really well.
- What would prompt you to actually investigate it more fully?
- What might be the benefit of such an investigation?
- How could you use the evidence emerging from the investigation in order to develop your teaching?

Something more than a straightforward evaluation will be needed, though, if you are to understand what is going on in a more fundamental sense or appreciate why an innovation has worked well. It is one thing to successfully evaluate a development; it is something quite else for other educators to find insights in the study that will help them to re-frame their own practice or to make changes that will improve the learning of their own students. This, after all, is one of the key reasons why people conduct educational research, so that one can see things quite differently.

AND THEN MOVING INTO RESEARCH

What this means is that a move into educational research places genuine demands on the researcher. It is naïve to imagine that you can just wander into rigorous explorations of why an innovation has worked or how it challenges assumptions about the purpose of education in different contexts. Nonetheless, lecturers from some disciplines may well find it easier to move into educational research than those from other disciplines.

Tutors with a background in the social sciences may well have an advantage over those in other disciplines, given the locus of their academic expertise. Research into learning and teaching typically offers conclusions that are relatively limited in extent, given the unpredictability of human behaviour and the myriad of concerns that actually shape day-to-day practice. Academics from the natural sciences, certainly, will be used to drawing conclusions that are more definitive in nature, and they are likely to need to adjust to the difference. Similarly, they made need to adjust to the use of qualitative research methods, as these methods can help to capture the complexity of educational experience. In Case study 8.2 Neill Thew looks at his own entry into educational research.

Case study 8.2
FIRST STEPS INTO RESEARCH

Neill Thew, Cru Leader Development (*formerly* University of Sussex)

How did I adapt to a new research paradigm when I first began to engage in research into my teaching? I think that the honest answer has to be slowly, hesitantly, painfully, and with many false starts. Like many of us moving into a new research area, I didn't really know for quite some time what it was that I didn't know.

My academic background is in English literature and psychoanalysis. Give me a text, and I'm in comfortably familiar territory. However, I still vividly remember attending my first teaching and learning – as opposed to English Studies – conference. My two lasting impressions are a sense of panic that I was a total fraud being there at all – half expecting at any moment to be exposed and booted out – and that the tone of the conference was considerably more collegial and less combative than I was used to.

My route into researching my own teaching was perhaps unusual. As a literary critic, I was interested in identities – what they were; how they came into being; and how they were subject to sometimes vicious contestation and debate. I came to realise that some of the same processes relating to ethnicity and gender that I was analysing in texts were being played out before me in my classrooms, and that my own presence and behaviours were significantly involved in these dynamics. I found this insight personally hugely challenging, and could not leave it alone.

My first steps, then, were to see what research skills I could transfer from studying texts to investigating my classrooms, pedagogy and practices. I'm not sure quite how consciously planned this was: I was just, I think, reacting to wanting to explore an idea in the way that seemed natural to me. My research perspective was essentially invisible to me. I certainly wasn't explicitly asking myself any epistemological questions about the nature of the research, evidence or 'truth' I was exploring.

As time went on and I began to encounter the scholarly field, I was able to locate my work and research assumptions within a wider context. Given that we all come to researching our own teaching from any number of different directions, then the things that challenge or surprise us are likely to differ considerably. Every year, the Postgraduate Certificate in Higher Education participants with whom I now work are challenged in a huge variety of ways as they come to find themselves in a territory between their own discipline and investigating their teaching. My own three challenges were: encountering quantitative work for the first time, and not having a clue what these tests and columns of numbers really meant; being frustrated by what I read as an alarmingly prevalent apologetic tone in much teaching research; and having to grapple with the issue of finding myself an object of my own enquiry to a significantly greater degree than ever before (though, of course, working on identity had already required me to think carefully and systematically about my own).

One might be tempted just to go ahead and collect some data, perhaps related to assessment, and then to try to make sense of it in one way or another. A research design, though, needs to come at an early stage of the process, not least to ensure that the data you collect is appropriate to the issues you are specifically looking to investigate, issues that are usually given a focus in research questions. The data will need to be rich enough to explore the issues around *why* this educational practice is effective or inadequate; a central issue in the extent to which your work can be seen to apply to other situations. You can, of course, work your own way through a textbook on educational research methodology, such as Creswell (2017) or Robson and McCartan (2016), but mastering this on your own would require quite some dedication. Rigour is essential if you are to publish your research in an established educational journal. There are a good number of well-regarded journals that focus specifically on research into higher education, although there seems to be greater variation in the quality of the journal when the focus is on higher education in specific disciplines. Publication is, of course, possible in other places than in journals. The first teaching development that one of us carried out was intended as an action research project, but the underpinning methodology was weak, and the data that was collected proved insufficient: it never saw publication in a peer-reviewed journal. It failed as a research project, although not in development terms, leading to a study guide on mathematics and its applications that addresses the thinking processes that students need to master if they are to learn effectively in these disciplines (Kahn, 2001).

Gaining a master's degree (or even a doctorate) in an education-related discipline could make a significant difference to your capacity to grasp the expertise needed for educational research. You might think that understanding could be developed without so much jargon or abstruse theory, but this is much easier to claim than to deliver on! Theory can offer significant insight into why a given teaching strategy might be effective with students, or not. Taking care to define the meaning of one's terms is an important part of this. This does not mean that one need simply take existing theory for granted. There is a great deal to be said for taking a critical stance towards theories that are used to frame teaching and learning. Notions of deep and surface learning have come in for particular criticism (Howie & Bagnall, 2013), as has research on learning styles (Coffield, Moseley, Hall, and Ecclestone, 2004). There is good scope to critique the extensive use of constructive alignment as a basis for organising student learning (Kahn, 2015).

An educational qualification would help you to engage with this territory. You could seek to master this on your own, whether taking a Massive Open Online Course (MOOC) in educational research or locating relevant textbooks or online resources. Nonetheless, part-time master's degrees in education are relatively easy to find (do take a look and see if your own institution offers one, perhaps with progression onto it from a Postgraduate Certificate in learning and teaching), with many such degrees offered online or with residential elements if one is not available locally. The next case study outlines how Christopher Wiley opened up the possibility of engaging in pedagogic research through gaining an advanced teaching qualification, leading to a range of new openings within his career. He identifies significant gains in going beyond what is mandatory to learn how to research into your own teaching.

Case study 8.3
GOING THE EXTRA MILE WITH A POSTGRADUATE TEACHING QUALIFICATION

Christopher Wiley, Department of Music and Media, University of Surrey

Sitting in a vibrant classroom over a decade ago, on day one of the opening module of the MA in Academic Practice programme at City University London, I encountered electronic voting systems (EVSs) for the first time in a higher education setting. Little did I know the extent to which my pursuit of that degree would engage me with pedagogic theory and its practical application: it enriched many different areas of my teaching, facilitated my dissemination of original pedagogic research in various international forums, and ultimately led teaching to occupy a prominence within my career that I could not have anticipated when I entered the academic profession as Lecturer in Music.

That single session, for instance, inspired me to introduce EVSs within my lectures the very next week, as well as to explore the published literature examining different approaches to its usage. The years that followed saw me draw upon that combined real-world experience and scholarly knowledge in championing EVS widely, delivering teaching workshops at a dozen UK universities and addressing conferences across Europe. These endeavours came full circle when I was awarded funding to publish a report for the Higher Education Academy on my pioneering use of EVS in non-science-based subjects, thereby actively contributing to the same pedagogic discourse that had led to the enhancement of my academic practice in the first place.

Many academic-related staff I have encountered on postgraduate courses of this nature at a range of different institutions have either not sought to progress beyond the introductory module or have taken only the first 60 credits in order to gain the PGCert (or equivalent) qualification, often driven by the need to fulfil the stipulations of their probation. Conversely, my approach has been to proceed through the full Master's degree, in order to sustain my immersion in current research on education – starting, in my second year of the programme, by furthering my new-found enthusiasm for EVS.

This conscious alignment of my studies with focal points of my teaching career prompted a level of involvement with pedagogic research that in some cases extended significantly beyond the course itself. The module on academic leadership, which I had originally followed to support my assuming a major directorial role, resulted in a reflective essay that the examiners recommended I develop for publication. A couple of years later, an academic colleague came across my article and suggested that I investigate autoethnography as a possible research method. I have since published two further essays on the subject and recently organised an influential conference exploring autoethnography's potential within music studies, activating engagement in this rich area of pedagogic research for a variety of academics in my home discipline and paving the way for others similarly to improve their own teaching practice.

My pursuit of pedagogic scholarship paid many additional dividends in terms of career progression, leading to my appointment as Director of Learning and Teaching in the School of Arts at the University of Surrey, as well as to successful applications for the National Teaching Fellowship and for Senior and Principal Fellowship of the Higher Education Academy. While a teaching qualification may too often be regarded merely as mandatory training for a lecturing position, I found that I reaped significant gains from undertaking formal postgraduate study in terms of my continuing professional development and the transformative impact upon my academic practice. By reaching beyond the programme's minimum requirements to maintain my engagement with pedagogic research, a number of new teaching-related avenues opened up for my career, which in certain respects have even eclipsed my principal area of activity as an internationally acknowledged musicologist.

A qualification will be valuable on other grounds as well. The deadlines that come with educational qualifications do provide a spur to work, especially given that they cannot easily be avoided. If you are to sustain the demands that are entailed in learning there is a great deal to be gained from socialising the experience. This, after all, is one of the lessons that we hope this book has been able to drive home for you as an educator. This socialisation does usually come when taking a qualification – whether through a tutor, supervisor or peers. Even when one has an initial qualification, though, research of the very highest calibre or that has a wide-ranging impact usually takes something more.

SOCIALISING YOUR RESEARCH

World-leading research is usually conducted within research groups, or at least in the company of others. Universities are also increasingly encouraging researchers to focus on overarching themes, in the hope that synergies will result that lead to higher levels of funding or that raise the overall quality of research. There is some variation between disciplines, of course, but there has been a relentless growth in collaborative research over the years. If others are to learn from your research, there is a great deal to be said for co-construction of the innovation in the first place. The most effective way to disseminate a development is to involve those you would like to find out about the project right from the start. If colleagues actually contribute to what is planned they will certainly find out about what is going on, and are more likely to be ready to trial or adapt your materials and ideas. Of course, this is not always possible, but for maximum impact of a development this mindset is essential. It may be the case that colleagues have different priorities, nonetheless, given their own commitment to their discipline rather than to advancing the teaching of that discipline.

There are a myriad of ways, though, to socialise your research that extend beyond engaging in collaborative research. Some fascinating research by Brew, Boud, Namgung, Lucas and Crawford (2016) found that researchers who see their activity as a social phenomenon are likely to be more productive than those who see research as a series of tasks or a journey of discovery. They called this a trading conception of research, with publications exchanged for recognition or research grants secured for the associated prestige. Such a conception of research is seen to lead quite directly to identifying oneself as a researcher. They suggested that research develops most fully when one publishes, joins a network, collaborates with others or undertakes peer review. Researchers then recognise each other and cite each other. These activities also support a person's self-identification as a researcher, as well as higher levels of performance. And note that they also found that those holding a doctorate were more likely to hold a trading conception of research, perhaps having been socialised into this mindset during their doctoral studies.

O'Byrne (2011), meanwhile, investigated the emergence of researcher identity amongst lecturers in a teaching-focused institution. There are clear ways in which her analysis applies to any context in which there are relatively few colleagues engaged in the same area of research as oneself. She found that it is possible to counteract this negative structural placing through one's own initiative. Those who established themselves as high-quality researchers were either able to find or to found a group or network that was closely allied to their research. She termed these collectivities that provided the researcher with a conceptual home. Such a collectivity is a place where one is able to trade with others. Indeed, it was the 'non-researchers' in the study who just tried to make the best of their lot, and who made no attempt to start up their own research group. As authors, our own awareness of this publication by O'Byrne stemmed from a role that one of us held as an assistant editor on the journal that published it – an example of a trade, as it were.

Or take another example. Writing for publication is a demanding activity. Experts on writing (see for instance, Boice, 1990) suggest that you should build regular opportunities to write into your weekly schedule, rather than simply relying on a binge approach, as a more regular approach is easier to sustain in the longer run, and leads to higher levels of productivity. It will help in this if you can divide larger writing tasks into more manageable sub-tasks, and this in turn indicates a need to structure your writing early on. But it is still hard to make this time unless the writing is sufficiently important for you. One straightforward option is to aim for a publishing opportunity that has a deadline attached to it – whether it is an invitation to submit a paper for a special issue of a journal or a call for conference papers. It is surprising how much difference this can make in concentrating the mind – all because your writing has been socialised. Trading can make a difference here as well – there is a good deal to gain from finding someone who is willing to exchange comments on draft work with you. Why not try and found a research group in your own setting, focused on educational research? Or perhaps start with a reading group focused on one of the foci for collective practice that were outlined in Chapter 6?

Many of the points that have been made in earlier chapters about the value of relationships to establishing a discipline or to enhancing practice also apply to your capacity to engage in research. You might take the time to find a mentor for your educational research, or to join an action learning set focused on research into your practice.

Review point 8.2
TRADING AND NETWORKS

- What research products are you developing that you could trade with others? How might you go about making trades?
- What networks or groups are you connected to that relate to your research? What scope is there to extend your engagement with these, or to start a group of your own?

CONCLUSIONS

Research requires dedication. If this is all in addition to your research within your discipline, and to all the other duties that you have to carry out, then you can see why the transition from evaluation to educational research is a challenging one to make. Nonetheless, research into learning and teaching offers a real opportunity for you to become an excellent teacher. The public dimension to research may also enable you to establish a reputation for such teaching, opening up further opportunities to develop your teaching.

REFERENCES

Ashwin, P. & Trigwell, K. (2004). Investigating staff and educational development. In D. Baume & P. E. Kahn, *Enhancing Staff and Educational Development* (pp. 117–31). London: Routledge.

Boice, R. (1990). *Professors as Writers: A Self-Help Guide to Productive Writing* (Vol. 190). Stillwater, OK: New Forums Press.

Boyer, E. L. (1990). *Scholarship Reconsidered*. Princeton, NJ: Carnegie Foundation for the Advancement of Teaching.

Brannick, T. & Coghlan, D. (2007). In defense of being "native": The case for insider academic research. *Organizational Research Methods*, *10*(1), 59–74.

Brew, A., Boud, D., Namgung, S. U., Lucas, L. & Crawford, K. (2016). Research productivity and academics' conceptions of research. *Higher Education*, *71*(5), 681–97.

Coffield, F., Moseley, D., Hall, E. & Ecclestone, K. (2004). *Learning Styles and Pedagogy in Post-16 Learning: A Systematic and Critical Review*. London: Learning and Skills Research Centre.

Creswell, J. W. (2017). *Research Design: Qualitative, Quantitative, and Mixed Methods Approaches*. Thousand Oaks, CA: SAGE.

Gurin, P., Dey, E., Hurtado, S. & Gurin, G. (2002). Diversity and Higher Education: Theory and impact on educational outcomes. *Harvard Educational Review*, *72*(3), 330–67.

Hamilton, M. & Appleby, Y. (2009). Critical perspectives on practitioner research: introduction to the special edition. *Studies in the Education of Adults*, *41*(2), 107–17.

Howie, P. & Bagnall, R. (2013). A critique of the deep and surface approaches to learning model. *Teaching in Higher Education*, *18*(4), 389–400.

Kahn, P.E. (2001). *Studying Mathematics and Its Applications*. London: Palgrave.

Kahn, P.E. (2015). Critical perspectives on methodology in pedagogic research, *Teaching in Higher Education*, *20*(4), 442 – 54.

Kuh, G. D. & Schneider, C. G. (2008). *High-impact Educational Practices: What They Are, Who Has Access to Them, and Why They Matter*. Washington, DC: Association of American Colleges and Universities.

O'Byrne, C. (2011). Against the odds: researcher development in teaching-focused HEIs. *International Journal for Researcher Development*, *2*(1), 8–25.

Richardson, M., Abraham, C. & Bond, R. (2012). Psychological correlates of university students' academic performance: A systematic review and meta-analysis. *Psychological Bulletin*, *138*(2), 353.

Robson, C. & McCartan, K. (2016). *Real World Research*. Sussex: John Wiley & Sons.

Saunders, M. (2000). Beginning an evaluation with RUFDATA: theorizing a practical approach to evaluation planning. *Evaluation*, 6(1), 7–21.

Tamim, R. M., Bernard, R. M., Borokhovski, E., Abrami, P. C. & Schmid, R. F. (2011). What forty years of research says about the impact of technology on learning: A second-order meta-analysis and validation study. *Review of Educational Research*, 81(1), 4–28.

Trigwell, K. & Shale, S. (2004). Student learning and the scholarship of university teaching. *Studies in Higher Education*, 29(4), 523–36.

Chapter 9
Taking a lead in teaching

INTRODUCTION

Leadership makes a difference. People certainly notice when a leader has failed in his or her responsibilities, and good leadership can raise a group or institution to an entirely new level. Snowden and McSherry (2017) highlighted leadership as a key influence on excellence, but what is leadership and how can it best be exercised? It is important to remember, as Alvesson and Sveningsson (2003) have argued, that a notion such as 'leadership' is just that, a hypothetical construct. That means that it can be framed and taken forward in a dizzyingly wide range of ways.

One thing is quite remarkable in the literature on leadership: it is possible for a group of people to achieve excellence together even when the leaders exhibit markedly different approaches to leadership. Kok and McDonald (2017) identified a set of ways by which specific leadership practices were linked to high-performing academic departments in relation to both teaching and research, but there was no single set of leadership practices that were associated with high levels of performance. Gibbs, Knapper and Piccinin (2008) similarly saw that markedly different approaches to leadership nonetheless still led to teaching excellence. However, in both studies it was clear that leadership of one kind or another was pivotal in whether the department as a whole came to be characterised as excellent at teaching. There is a great deal to be gained from investing in leadership if the support for learning that your students receive is to let you stand out from the crowd.

There are many ways to exercise leadership, but its nature does shift when it is carried out within a formally recognised role. Chapter 6 has already effectively addressed informal approaches to leadership. Taking on a role that allows you to lead the development of teaching within your institution, however, can increase your scope to initiate change. Your ideas may be taken more seriously, and you will have greater scope to shape the way in which they are implemented. Leadership roles that relate to teaching are often avoided as assiduously as possible, but what hope then for enhanced teaching on a collective level? Given this, it will help first of all to highlight briefly the kinds of roles that are available and how one might secure one. We will then go on to look in more detail at a set of practical and actionable ways to exercise leadership.

SECURING A ROLE

The list of teaching responsibilities is a long and familiar one. Leadership responsibilities can come at module, programme, departmental, school, faculty or university level. Responsibilities might be focused on the curriculum, learning technology, assessment, inclusion, quality enhancement, student welfare, postgraduate research and so on. Higher education has high levels of autonomy relative to other employment sectors, and this is manifested in part in the leadership roles that are open to staff at all kinds of levels. Positions come up regularly within departments, whether as a quality assurance lead, disability support coordinator, dean of students, director of postgraduate research and so on. Roles offer varying scope for the development of teaching and lead to different outcomes, though, so it may make sense to target some roles and avoid others. Has the role previously been framed with maintenance or change in mind? What scope would there be to redefine the role if you were to take it on?

You can't assume that senior colleagues will automatically share your own perspectives on the areas in which you might be well placed to take a lead. A model that is helpful in analysing awareness within the process of human interaction is the Johari Window, as outlined in Figure 9.1. This window describes four different aspects of awareness: the open area, which represents things that I know about myself and that others know about me; the blind area, representing things that others know about me but which I myself am blind to; the hidden area, for things that I know about myself but do not reveal to others; and finally the unknown area, containing things of which neither I nor others are aware. It is easy to assume that the open area is larger than it actually is, as much of what we imagine is known to others is in fact hidden from them. The challenge

	Known to self	Not known to self
Known to others	**Open area**	**Blind area**
Not known to others	**Hidden area**	**Unknown area**

FIGURE 9.1 The Johari Window, after Luft (1970)

then is to develop the trust needed to be more open with our colleagues, and when appropriate with our students as we saw earlier in Chapter 3, about our motivations, experiences, attitudes, values and so on.

Review point 9.1
ASSESSING YOUR KNOWLEDGE

1. Choose three different aspects of your teaching where you have particular interest, ability or experience, and assess the scope that each aspect offers for taking on further responsibility.

2. Complete a Johari window for the most promising of these three aspects, by assessing how much knowledge is present in each area of the window (except of course for the 'Unknown area'!), and by providing examples of knowledge contained within each area. For the 'Blind area' you will clearly need help from one or more colleagues. If you subsequently revisit this exercise you should be able to reduce the size of the unknown area.

3. How can you increase the trust with your colleagues that fosters disclosure of your hidden knowledge? How can you gain feedback on your work in this area from your colleagues?

A further option is to actually create your own role, perhaps on the basis of an innovative approach to student learning. Derrick Chong in Case study 9.1 volunteered to take on leadership of a marketing module entailing a large class of studies. Work in a more junior role opened up a pathway into a senior leadership role on teaching within his School.

Case study 9.1
"I AM TITANIUM": AN ANTHEM FOR NEW COURSE DEVELOPMENT

Derrick Chong, School of Management, Royal Holloway, University of London

I wrote the lyrics from David Guetta's Titanium (2011) on the back page of a Muji A5 notebook – purchased four months before the start of the 2013/14 academic year – as the credo to buoy my spirits. I had offered to lead and design a new, mandatory, first-year marketing course (425 students). The proposed course title Markets and Consumption had met with resistance from colleagues involved with undergraduate recruitment who believed that 'Marketing' ought to feature.

In addition to Guetta's anthem – put it on when you want to be the very best – various techniques at different stages were adopted to develop confidence in trying something new. First, backstage work in collaborating with faculty to agree Markets and Consumption as reflecting our shared research interests. This meant collective ownership with a commitment to research-led/informed pedagogy that introduces students to a more realistic image of marketing in society. Thus a socio-political approach with links to cogent disciplines. Second, preparation work was needed before teaching. This is about allowing sufficient time, over a period of months, to think and plan the organisational structure. The A5 notebook was a portable and convenient way to record impulses on lectures, workshops, assessment topics, assigned readings, etc. Writing is a record of the creative process, of how early versions evolve. Third, effective delivery to a large class includes reinforcing clear signposts. Doing so recognises that Markets and Consumption would be one of their first courses at university.

There were no bullets to ricochet. Forms of feedback validated the decision to view teaching practice in a new light. Separate external examiners have commended the curriculum design: 'I welcome the strong critical and societal elements of the module topics' (2013/14); and 'The introduction of critical perspectives in marketing to first-year students including the role of marketing theory is a strength' (2015/16). Moreover, course feedback from students has been positive, including being student-nominated – 'magnificent in organising and delivering interactive lectures that are engaging and stimulating' and 'an approach to lectures led to students engaging well with his course' – for a College Excellence in Service Award in 2016. Emergent learning via self-reflection and feedback, from students and workshop tutors, has informed the active revision of each subsequent edition.

> Nominating myself to develop a new course has been an opportunity to refresh and enliven my teaching. Markets and Consumption enabled me to rethink my approach to marketing. Collaborating with colleagues reinforced the collective nature of curriculum design. Jotting things down in the A5 notebook was an instructive way to shape and control the flow of ideas. In addition, there have been benefits to professional development: scholarship via published pedagogic research; and academic administration such as being appointed the School of Management's Director of Undergraduate Studies and Senior Tutor.

Taking the initiative in this way allows you greater control over your future development path, and being able to demonstrate that you are actively involved in a number of roles can also help in avoiding being 'volunteered' for potentially less desirable positions! It is true that some roles offer greater scope to make a name for yourself: establishing a new master's degree programme may count for more than keeping the students happy who are already there. If colleagues can see that you have the capacity to introduce new initiatives, then it is quite possible that you will be given further rein to carry out development work, perhaps without the administrative load that is attached to more established responsibilities.

TAKING ON LEADERSHIP

At some point you are likely to actually take on a specific role that allows you scope to develop teaching, even if the role is not one that you initially wanted. A responsibility for teaching can, however, easily become a maintenance function rather than an occasion for leadership. The difference resides in the way that you carry out a role rather than the role itself. Even what you might think of as mundane roles can allow scope for development opportunities. Leadership entails someone defining the world within which others operate. It takes more than working budgets, being determined in meetings and introducing new standard operating procedures. The rest of this chapter focuses on a set of practical leadership strategies.

Setting out an agenda for leadership

A clear vision of where you want things to end up is important. Awareness of the direction of travel, and a sense that this matters is an integral part of this. While their research focused on a fairly conventional view of excellence, Kok and McDonald (2017) found that top departments had a clear sense of direction that was expressed in collectively agreed goals. A well-judged agenda for change is essential, one that is grounded in an understanding of what makes for effective learning. But the range of possible directions in which you can develop your teaching remains vast. Which ideas should you prioritise? Should you focus on assessment, the accessibility of your internet resources, the extent to which you foster a dialogue with your students? Or perhaps it is more important to introduce some recent research into a stale course unit. It may help to engage in a strategic planning process, modelled on Ramsden (1998):

Situation analysis

- What are the institutional or national trends that underpin change related to your role?
- Spell out the characteristics of the environment in which your role is situated. What interests and motivates your colleagues?

Outcome analysis

- What student learning needs are in most urgent need of attention?
- What do you want to achieve in this role? For yourself, for specific colleagues and for your team as a whole?
- What would colleagues and managers want you to achieve in this role?

Leadership agenda

- What is the gap between your current situation and the desired outcome?
- Set out your leadership agenda in light of the gap between these, detailing your priorities, strategies, dangers to avoid, and development needs.

Kezar and Carducci (2007) suggested that work is needed on short-term and long-term goals at the same time, if one is to keep colleagues motivated and shift embedded practices. Early on, you might also introduce initiatives that mean you need to spend less time maintaining systems.

Time spent on processes rather than content can be particularly beneficial, as even introducing a simple proforma or standard letter can streamline a process, or allow a task to be passed on to someone else. You may then only need to review the process rather than carry it out each time.

Awareness of the research literature can be an essential aspect of this. An example of practice which puts the student at the heart of the process, and is still efficient in staff time, can have a compelling effect on colleagues. In setting your agenda it is important to have a keen awareness of the possible practice that you might adopt. Leadership builds on one's own command of practice. We see in the next case study by Linda Altshul that interest in a particular research area led to a school-wide agenda for change. Engagement with research can also help you to adopt a critical take on leadership. Whose interests are being served by the direction in which you are taking practice? Does your agenda marginalise anyone?

Case study 9.2
HOW THE TEAM OF TEACHERS RAN

Linda Altshul, School of Languages, University of Salford

We had three parallel classes running; and how the team of teachers ran! At the end of each tutored self-access class on the English as a Foreign Language programme we were left exhilarated by the buzz from the interaction. We started each class separately with a short activity to widen learner awareness of possible approaches to studying a particular language skill. Then students chose a task and could study in any of four equipped self-access rooms, with the tutors advising and answering questions. Each session ended with a whole-group review of what had been learned.

This approach had emerged from my interest in the growing international research and practice in self-access language learning that I had learned about during my own postgraduate studies. After collecting and disseminating evidence of the benefits, I was asked to co-ordinate a working group to develop the programme. I introduced the team-teaching described above to enable on-going training for teachers who were new to the ideas. We had staff development workshops and regular meetings, both face-to-face and via email. Other teachers contributed ideas to the development of the programme as their own enthusiasm and experience grew. The programme became known as DILL — Developing Independent Language Learning.

The growing success of DILL and the opening of the multi-media Language Resource Centre led to a request by the Head of School that I should make a proposal to widen and adapt the application to the whole school through personal tutoring. His authority backed up my recommendations, which were accepted. I was asked to chair the school-wide working group that rolled out DILL to all languages students. Concurrently I made a successful bid for external funding to look into the effects of DILL on student progression and retention. This bought time so that I could increase staff development activities across the school and also enabled making DILL materials available on a virtual learning environment (VLE).

The effects of the DILL approach are radical not only with the learners, but also with staff. While there remains a minority who have yet to be convinced, DILL has introduced many colleagues to a learner-centred approach. A typical tutor said, 'I felt a bit out of my depth' during the first year. However, confidence and skills have grown through both experience and an extensive staff development programme, which colleagues now help to lead. Another tutor's comment exemplifies the impact of the DILL programme: 'The interest is in seeing how students think. The closer we can get to their view of how they are learning, the better we can teach — or rather get them to learn.'

My role in advancing staff development and use of e-learning led to a secondment as Faculty Learning Technologies Fellow. I now continue to promote a learner-centred focus in use of the VLE in other disciplines in the training sessions that I run across the faculty.

Teaching is typically based around local, collegial contexts that are defined on the basis of disciplinary expertise. Mårtensson and Roxå (2016) referred to leaders in these contexts as 'local leaders'. They argued that this level is a key locus for excellence in teaching in higher education. They suggested that for local leadership to be effective, a careful balance needs to be struck between one's internal and external mandates. It is no good executing an agenda that is externally derived if one's colleagues are not willing to take you fully seriously as a leader. What this also suggests is that local leaders will need practices that enable them to span across boundaries (Prysor and Henley, 2017) if they are to realise their leadership agenda and establish shared commitments and direction across boundaries. Don't remain holed up within your own limited world!

Realising your leadership agenda

Articulating an agenda for change is one thing, but what are the concrete means by which you can deliver it? What will it take to realise this vision – or to realise somewhere like it? Kezar and Carducci (2007) argued that our underlying notions of leadership in Western cultures are predicated around notions of controlling others, but that we need to move toward a greater awareness of the value of a collectively oriented change process. What would induce someone to spend their time on your project or concerns rather than on an agenda of their own? What will your colleagues be willing to join with, and that still fits your agenda for the short and long term?

Strategy communication

It is important to communicate one's agenda in a way that catalyses the interest and engagement of others. Kok and McDonald (2017) found that top departments were ready to embrace change, and that they reported more frequent and formalised communication than lower performing departments between the head of department and staff within the department. One's leadership narrative and strategy needs to be shared with others:

- How much time are you willing to spending on communicating with those you would like to be influenced by your leadership, and in what ways? What communication channels are open to you? How could you take better advantage of these?
- Bring your agenda to all the contexts within which you operate, at team meetings, professional development reviews, seminars and so on. Make decisions transparently in light of it.
- How can you articulate your vision in a compelling fashion? There is a case for story telling at times in getting your message across, especially when making a presentation. Hunt down stories that relate to your leadership, whether from your own experience or that you encounter on the way.

Review point 9.2
STAYING IN TOUCH

- Identify some specific ways by which you can stay more closely in touch with those who are affected by your leadership.

Distributing leadership

Bolden, Petrov and Gosling (2009) suggested that there is something of a consensus in the literature on leadership in universities that it should be distributed. Distributed leadership entails either senior leaders devolving some aspects of leadership to others or new leaders emerging through bottom-up influence. They suggested, though, that the actual means by which leadership is distributed have received little attention:

- The distributed nature of leadership in higher education is given focus partly through a range of roles. Indeed, this represents one strategy for those in more senior leadership roles. Roles provide a focus for your colleagues to take the initiative.
- What roles would be helpful in realising your vision? Map out all of the roles that already come under your responsibility. How could you reconfigure these roles in support of your leadership agenda or introduce new roles?

There may still be some scope to drive through your own agenda more forcefully in a top-down fashion, but this will depend on your level of authority and influence – and on your capacity to control resources and rewards.

Promote good working relations

Hempsall (2014) suggested that a strong focus on ensuring good quality relationships is essential for leadership. Do you trust each other? Is there work in common that will provide a basis for this trust to develop? Can you find ways to ensure shared areas of responsibility or overlapping responsibilities where some negotiation is required? Capacity for development is related to your ability to create links with other people, as Gustavsen (2001) argued. He pointed out that new ideas are often stimulated by discussions or work with others, as are strategies to overcome challenges in development work. The richer and denser are your relationships with others in the field, the greater the fund of ideas on which to draw – as we noted earlier in Chapter 6.

In the case study that follows Danijela Serbic considers the importance of supporting the colleagues for whom she is providing leadership. She looks at ways to work with Graduate Teaching Assistants, colleagues who can play a particularly important role in helping to sustain high levels of teaching intensity.

Case study 9.3
HELPING POSTGRADUATE TUTORS TO BECOME SKILLED AND CONFIDENT TEACHERS

Danijela Serbic, Department of Psychology, Royal Holloway,
University of London

Taking a lead in teaching can take many forms, from leading teaching activities to mentoring junior colleagues. Junior teaching staff are an integral part of a number of modules that I teach and co-ordinate. In this case study, I will specifically focus on one module that I co-ordinate, Psychology Undergraduate Seminars. The main aim of the module is to enable students to develop their critical thinking skills by evaluating psychological research and theory. All seminars are taught by postgraduate tutors (PhD students).

Last year, I co-ordinated a team of five PhD students, four of whom were in their first year of their PhD and had no prior teaching experience. Being a postgraduate tutor only a few years ago, helped me put myself into their shoes and work out a support plan for them. Teaching seminars is all about small group teaching, therefore I began with a group training session, where I shared with them skills that are needed for effective small group teaching. We discussed topics such as how to encourage and balance student contributions and participation in class discussions, and how to deal with students' questions and queries. But, in order to address the tutors' unique needs and utilise their strengths, it is also important to implement personalised leadership. Hence, I ensured that they received personalised support by meeting with them individually, listening to them and ensuring that they feel their work is respected and valued. They responded well to this, for example I was asked by some tutors to observe their teaching and provide feedback.

Teaching seminars does not require postgraduate tutors to prepare teaching materials or contribute to the module development; their role is to deliver seminars. In spite of this, I ensure that the tutors get experience of how a module develops so that they can contribute to this process. I help them increase their ownership of seminars, leadership skills and independence by involving them in the design and preparation of seminar materials. For example, last year they were given the opportunity to work as a team on revamping and redesigning a whole seminar. All tutors enthusiastically embraced this opportunity and organised themselves to redesign the seminar. I also ensure that the tutors are actively involved in any further developments of the module by asking for their suggestions and feedback. Increasing tutors' ownership of seminars empowered them, greatly influenced their involvement and enthusiasm, and they received overwhelmingly positive student feedback, with 100 per cent of qualitative comments relating to their teaching being positive. Our hard work and achievements were recognised by the college and resulted in a teaching prize, which was awarded in recognition of our effective and transferable approach to fostering student engagement.

Sustained and effective leadership of junior colleagues can contribute immensely to their development of becoming skilled and confident teachers. Assisting and guiding them in this process is an extremely rewarding experience that I would highly recommend to university lecturers who are looking to develop their leadership skills, and that recently enabled me to obtain the Senior Fellowship of the Higher Education Academy.

Personal underpinnings of leadership

Leadership can place significant strains on leaders. A tenacity in seeking what is important for the department is thus a key trait of a leader. Are you tempted to give up on your agenda for change? If you meet a setback, what are the options for working around the challenge? Of course, one can annoy a senior leader through such persistence, but if the occasions on which one asks are well judged this should be less of a concern. Kazar and Carducci (2007) argued that leaders need their own sources of renewal if they are to stay tenacious in front of setbacks or opposition. What are your own sources of inner renewal?

It will also be worth paying attention to time management – and to creating space to allow you to shape the role in light of your priorities, rather than reacting passively to day-to-day demands. You may thus find it helpful to adopt a range of time management exercises, developing your ability to manage your workload. Perhaps the first most important aspect of time management is actually to be aware of how you spend your time; does it reflect your priorities? You will also find that if you continually move from one task to another, perhaps by accessing emails, taking phone calls or browsing the internet too frequently, then you will benefit from planning what you carry out when, and then protecting your plans. This can allow you to plan in key activities that otherwise might never happen, such as reading articles or other material related to the development side of your role, and to deliver on your priorities. Most staff in higher education fulfil a number of roles, making it important to manage your workload as a whole, an issue that the final case study by Julie Wray explores.

Case study 9.4
BALANCING MY WORKLOAD

Julie Wray, School of Nursing, University of Salford

When I first came into higher education four years ago I was confident that I would be able to balance my teaching with everything else entailed in a lecturing role. My development would just happen, as I was both crafted at reflexivity and experienced in research. Having come direct from healthcare practice I felt capable of meeting the challenges, organising my workload and being assertive about saying no.

Well, maybe no surprise that this did not happen. Within a year the demands of the job had overwhelmed me, and I was bogged down in what seemed like boring, cluttered and uncreative work. I was constantly problem solving for students, and burdened by paperwork and the need to comply with University rules (and there are plenty). There seemed to be little time left even to plan my teaching, let alone read the relevant literature or develop anything. I was leading a Master's programme, and yet had no space to organise and develop the programme. My output of publications had considerably depleted in comparison to when I was in practice; and this certainly felt rather odd. I began to wonder how this had all happened.

It occurred to me after looking at my yearly workload-balance form that most of my time was spent on jobs that were allocated the lowest weighting. This was largely down to an aspect of my practice that I was not really equipped to deal with: my role as a problem-based learning (PBL) facilitator. This form of teaching was new to me, and whilst I attended some training sessions and read the literature, actual practice of PBL with students proved overpowering. I had become consumed by their inability to work as a team and create a cohesive group dynamic, and had begun to adopt an approach to pastoral care that was far too matriarchal and 'hands on'.

I began to think about what strategies could be employed to enable the students to engage more appropriately in PBL and at the same time release me from a 'dependency role'. In talking to some students it struck me that they needed to take ownership and through this realisation I was able to pull back and hand over PBL to the students. I began, for instance, to timetable my availability and I requested from students a clear purpose for any meetings. I had seen my role as a teacher as being to teach and lost sight of the process of learning and discovery. As well as improving my teaching, this has created more time to dedicate to the masters programme and to my research.

Review point 9.3
TIME MANAGEMENT

Complete a log of how you spend your time for a week, indicating how long each task that you complete takes, as well as whether you had planned to carry it out.

And even if in practice one's teaching or administrative load is not fully adjusted to reflect the demands of the role, or not even adjusted at all, a clear responsibility does at least provide a reason to channel energy in the direction of developing your teaching.

CONCLUSIONS

Teaching offers immense scope for exercising leadership in proposing and implementing new ideas, drawing colleagues into the process and seeing the difference that your work can make for students. You clearly need to take responsibility for this process, deciding where and how to invest your effort, and where to hold back; perhaps staking your claim to an area through clearly recognised dynamism.

It is essential to learn to lead. There is a market for leadership courses in higher education, so do look at what might be available to you, and supported by your institution. There is also value in taking up opportunities for coaching, mentoring and action learning. It is one thing to recognise that leadership can be both socialised and charismatic, as Howell and Shamir (2005) have argued. It is quite another thing to deliver on it.

 REFERENCES

Alvesson, M. & Sveningsson, S. (2003). The great disappearing act: Difficulties in doing 'leadership'. *The Leadership Quarterly*, *14*(3), 359–81.

Bolden, R., Petrov, G., & Gosling, J. (2009). Distributed leadership in higher education: Rhetoric and reality. *Educational Management Administration & Leadership*, *37*(2), 257–77.

Gibbs, G., Knapper, C., & Piccinin, S. (2008). Disciplinary and contextually appropriate approaches to leadership of teaching in research-intensive academic departments in higher education. *Higher Education Quarterly*, 62(4), 416–36.

Gustavsen, B. (2001). Theory and practice: The mediating discourse. In P. Reason & H. Bradbury, *Handbook of Action Research: The Concise Paperback Edition* (pp. 17–26). Thousand Oaks, CA: SAGE.

Hempsall, K. (2014). Developing leadership in higher education: Perspectives from the USA, the UK and Australia. *Journal of Higher Education Policy and Management*, 36(4), 383–94.

Howell, J. M. & Shamir, B. (2005). The role of followers in the charismatic leadership process: Relationships and their consequences. *Academy of Management Review*, 30(1), 96–112.

Kezar, A. & Carducci, R. (2007). Cultivating revolutionary educational leaders: Translating emerging theories into action. *Journal of Research on Leadership Education*, 2(1), 1–46.

Kok, S. K. & McDonald, C. (2017). Underpinning excellence in higher education – an investigation into the leadership, governance and management behaviours of high-performing academic departments. *Studies in Higher Education*, 42(2), 210–31.

Luft, J. (1970). *The Johari Window: A Graphic Model of Awareness in Relations*. Palo Alto, CA: National Press Books.

Mårtensson, K. & Roxå, T. (2016). Leadership at a local level – Enhancing educational development. *Educational Management Administration & Leadership*, 44(2), 247–62.

Prysor, D. & Henley, A. (2017). Boundary spanning in higher education leadership: identifying boundaries and practices in a British university. *Studies in Higher Education*, 1–16.

Ramsden, P. (1998). *Learning to Lead in Higher Education*. London: Routledge.

Snowden, M. & McSherry, R. (2017). Establishing excellence: Where do we go from here? In *The Pedagogy of the Social Sciences Curriculum* (pp. 107–18). Switzerland: Springer.

Chapter 10

Understanding teaching excellence

INTRODUCTION

In 2007, the Higher Education Academy annual conference carried a motion that 'excellence has become a meaningless concept' (Skelton, 2009: 107). Since then, how much has changed? The sector has been caught up with attempts to get to the heart of what excellence *is*; and perhaps more importantly (or more disconcertingly depending on your perspective) how to *measure* it. Whatever 'it' is. This work has involved several commissioned literature reviews (including Little, Locke, Parker and Richardson, 2007; Gunn and Fisk, 2013), many books and articles (including Skelton, 2005, 2009; Su and Wood, 2012; Wood and Su, 2017), and much debate across the sector. While all this has been going on, politicians and subsequently our own institutions have decided to articulate that definition for us through a plethora of activity that has produced international global rankings, national league tables, student satisfaction surveys and frameworks, and in the UK, the apogee that is the Teaching Excellence Framework (TEF).

It feels as if we're missing a stage.

> Stage 1 – overwhelming focus on the concept of teaching excellence. Tick.
> Stage 3 – attempts made to measure teaching excellence. Tick.
> But what happened to Stage 2, *understanding* teaching excellence? The response would have to be: could do better.

Despite the work that has been done in this area 'ambiguities and contention around the definitions of teaching excellence, teacher excellence and their relationship to excellent student learning' (Gunn and Fisk, 2013: 6) still exist. Why does it continue to be so challenging?

UNDERSTANDING TEACHING EXCELLENCE

Take a moment to think about any definitions of excellence that exist in your institution. There are probably criteria-based teaching awards for excellence. If you're based in the UK, you may be working in an institution which has secured TEF Gold – or not; a result of institutional ranking around criteria for excellence. We award marks to students that can be rated as excellent against assessment marking scales. Promotion structures utilise the concept of excellence to differentiate between levels of performance, to allow some to progress and others not (yet). Definitions of teaching excellence are therefore all around us in some shape or form, providing a target to aim for, a gateway to success or a barrier to progress. Reflected in league tables it allows our institutions to jostle for the limelight and provides a potent attractant for all potential stakeholders. Excellence is an undeniably powerful construct; yet, are we actually any closer to *understanding* what excellence is and how we might use this understanding to help to inform and develop our teaching? This chapter will take a critical approach to the idea of excellence as it is used in contemporary higher education and consider ways in which a better understanding of the concept can help us to work with it to develop our teaching.

EXPLORING TEACHING EXCELLENCE

As discussed in Chapter 7, looking at drivers for teaching development, the sector is awash with tools and approaches to measure anything that is stamped 'higher education'. Many of these either explicitly or by inference claim to be measuring excellence. As a result, 'excellence' has become the accepted norm of institutional endeavour. Some of this is the result of attempts to align teaching excellence with research excellence as if the two could be matched step for step, rather than viewed as complementary aspects of professional practice. This approach has been a deliberate construct in the UK that has resulted in the government-initiated TEF but a brief search for the phrase 'teaching excellence' on the websites of universities worldwide also indicates that the concept has become a universal given in terms of institutional expectations (see also Wood and Su, 2017).

In order to help us explore the nature of teaching excellence we're going to approach it through a number of reflective questions in order to help us interrogate our practice. You might think of some others, specific to your own context, which you can contribute to this list.

- Is being excellent a skill, an attribute or an attitude to practice?
- Is the real and meaningful locus of excellence in the teaching or in the learning?
- Is excellent teaching practice an end in itself, or is it genuinely transferable?

Is being excellent a skill, an attribute or an attitude to practice?

There are a number of models and approaches aimed at explaining the development towards excellence, which have been posited in relation to skills acquisition and professional development. These include Benner's (1984) model focused on the journey from novice to expert in the nursing profession; Dreyfus and Dreyfus (1986); and Michael Eraut's (1994) work in relation to the development of professional competence. Ideas from this collection of work continue to resonate. Ray Land and George Gordon (2015: 5) outline an adapted version of the Dreyfus and Dreyfus categories (1986) in their report on international teaching excellence initiatives. In this, they outline 'levels of excellence' from competence, through proficiency to advanced proficiency and then to expertise or high recognition. Land and Gordon's work is presented in Table 10.1 in relation to that of Benner and Dreyfus and Dreyfus.

TABLE 10.1 Models of skills acquisition in the development of excellence

Benner's Model (1984)	Dreyfus & Dreyfus Model (1986)	Land & Gordon Model (2015)
Novice	Novice	
Advanced Beginner		
Competent	Competent	Competent (pre-condition of excellence)
Proficient	Proficient	Proficient
		Advanced Proficiency
Expert	Expert	Expertise/high recognition
	Mastery	

While both Benner and Dreyfus and Dreyfus identify a novice stage of skills development, the situation of Land and Gordon's work within the landscape of higher education teaching assumes a base level of competence which rises to expertise; a stage recognised by both Benner and Dreyfus and Dreyfus and only exceeded by mastery in the Dreyfus and Dreyfus model. None of the models articulates excellence as a separate category in its own right, with the implication being that excellence is developed throughout this journey of skills development as a process, rather than an end in itself. Expertise as a concept, and its relationship to excellence, is addressed later in this chapter in a think piece by Helen King.

Skill, proficiency and mastery in teaching are undeniably part of what contributes to teaching excellence but present a somewhat reductionist view of what is a highly complex concept. Our understanding of teaching relationships with students and their involvement in the teaching and learning process means that, as Su and Wood (2012: 142) argue, 'definitions of teaching excellence cannot be adequately obtained from typologies and descriptions of techniques and skills' but rather that 'student engagement in dialogue' is required to achieve teaching excellence. Su and Wood (2012: 143) also comment on 'conceptions of teaching as virtuous practice involving a complex interplay of emotion, "passion" and what we might call a certain indefinable "something" . . . [that] eludes measurement.'

This 'indefinable something' is the reason why programmes in academic practice are so much more than simply 'tips for teaching' and instead are based on reflective practice and engagement with the literature; it's why we are encouraged as teachers to develop our own personal philosophy of teaching, that becomes and remains a living touchstone throughout our careers; and it's why we are encouraged by frameworks such as the UKPSF to reflect on our professional values in addition to our core knowledge and our practical teaching activity. As Skelton notes (2009: 109): excellence is 'not simply about delivering a high quality performance or being better than others, it's about a process of struggle in concrete material circumstance'.

In the following case study, Roisin Donnelly, from the Dublin Institute of Technology (DIT), discusses the conversations she has had around teaching excellence with university teachers undertaking the PG Diploma in Third Level Learning and Teaching at DIT. In it, the themes of teaching skills and attitudes are discussed as part of the developing learning journey.

Case study 10.1
HOW DO I KNOW?

Roisin Donnelly, Dublin Institute of Technology

We all doubt ourselves at times, and we all have bad days in the classroom! Asking any of the (mostly early career) academic staff who are undertaking this teaching qualification what makes them excellent in their teaching role, generally begets the response: *'it's many things, working in tandem'*, and they can list the main characteristics of an excellent teacher fairly easily. Their responses generally echo those from the study by Su and Wood (2012) who report that it's a combination of the lecturer's willingness to help students and inspirational teaching methods that help make a good university teacher; being humorous and able to provide speedy feedback are an added bonus. In pursuing their teaching qualification, these diploma participants report that thinking about what is effective as well as what isn't can help them clarify how to improve professional teaching practice. Looking at what has not worked for them, and why (were they just having a bad day?) makes for interesting conversations! And asking them to delve deeper to consider how all this can be measured adds a richness to their teaching portfolios.

To secure this teaching qualification, these teachers are finding ways to plan their lessons, assess their students in a variety of authentic ways, listen to

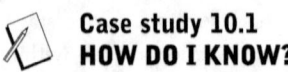

What makes me an excellent teacher?   How do I know?   Why is my class not working?

FIGURE 10.1 How do I know?

and collaborate with their students, and network with colleagues. They tweet, use technology, and try to inspire creative and critical thinking. Asking them to try to measure how they make decisions in and out of the classroom about all this, and more, and what impact those decisions have on what their students learn, is a pivotal part of their learning on the programme. Their discussions on what signifies excellent teaching seem to have less to do with their subject knowledge and skills than with their attitude toward their students, their subject, and their approach to how they work. Arguably, such teaching does not have templates or boundaries.

- Having an open attitude, a willingness to 'give it a go' and be flexible is what I draw upon when a class isn't working.
- Trying new things, shifting gears and evaluating my teaching throughout the class.
- Finding new ways to present material to make sure that every student understands the key concepts.
- All my students are asking questions, not just giving answers, and feel comfortable doing so.
- I listened as often as I have lectured.
- When I do all this, I know I've made an impact.

Being an excellent teacher is a challenge to achieve consistently, made more difficult by trying to gauge how we as teachers make decisions in the classroom, and what impact those decisions have on what and how our students learn. Exploring indicators that focus these efforts on what works and what doesn't for our own context can enhance our practice and our students' learning.

Review point 10.1
SKILLS AND ATTITUDES

Consider where you are in relation to the development of your skills as a teacher. This might be in relation to curriculum design, technology enhanced learning or effectively facilitating a class. Now reflect on your attitude to your teaching and your students. This can be gauged in terms of your levels of connection with your students, an understanding of where they've come from and where they want to go, and your developing relationship with them.

- In which of these areas, skills or attitudes, do you feel you are most developed?
- Which matters most to your development of excellent teaching; and which to your students in their learning?

It may be both equally, or you may feel that one has the edge over the other. Think about this the next time you are working with your students and what it tells you about excellent teaching.

Is the real and meaningful locus of excellence in the teaching or in the learning?

One of the more contentious aspects of the excellence debate is where it is situated. Is it in the institution, the teachers or the students? Is it in the culture or the environment? Or is it none of these, and actually it is in the products and outputs of university achievement, in its teaching, its learning and its research? And if we decide on it residing in any one or more of these loci then what does that mean for developing and understanding excellence? One of the main ways that the sector aims to understand excellence is by trying to measure it. However, the current focus on measurement of teaching excellence can distract from the heart of the matter by placing emphasis solely on measurable outcomes rather than developmental processes. As Wood and Su (2017: 461) comment: 'There is a saying that "weighing the pig doesn't make it fatter", and therefore the focus on outcome measures and indicators does not necessarily "improve" teaching.'

While the sector often refers to excellent teachers or excellent universities – and indeed rewards individuals and institutions on this basis – these are not necessarily helpful ideas for us when thinking about developing our own personal practice. And while they may encourage some to 'achieve more' through aligning their practice with award and recognition criteria, they can also prove dispiriting or frustrating for those of us working hard to develop our practice but who don't work in a university that has been rated excellent, or who haven't been recognised by an award or similar validation. It can make us question how much agency we have to develop excellence in our teaching, when the decisions about what constitutes excellence are defined by others.

Taking ownership of the concept of teaching excellence is an important step in its realisation within your practice. How can we do this? Look around you and think about where excellence is located in your immediate environment. Not just your department or faculty, and not even your colleagues: look at your students. Focusing our energies on developing an approach to excellence that supports achievement and attainment in student learning, can become our primary and arguably the best objective. It is an objective that will continue to change in light of the multifarious drivers that exist at any given time in relation to the student body, learner aspirations, political context and digital environment, etc., as we saw in Chapter 7; but it creates a definition of excellence in teaching that is aspirational and attainable.

Is excellent teaching practice an end in itself, or is it genuinely transferable?

Does teaching excellence have a 'sell by' date? If it is a concept that informs our teaching or inspires our teaching at any given point, and relates to specific criteria, does it follow that once achieved, excellence cannot remain as a permanent state or condition if the context or criteria change? This would appear to be the accepted definition of the state of excellence (as opposed to what it represents). Saunders and Blanco Ramirez (2017) refer to the 'relational' nature of excellence and Alan Skelton (2005) has described excellence as 'historically and situationally contingent'. Does this then mean that excellence and therefore excellent teaching is not transferable and not sustainable; and does this matter?

This view of excellence as transitory and individual is one that negatively impacts perceptions of teaching awards, recognition and reward schemes and frameworks that focus on excellence. As a result, many have found the concept of teaching awards to be problematic in relation to teaching excellence. Skelton (2009: 110) advises that we shouldn't be looking for teaching excellence as 'an essence within heroic individuals [as] it resides in the material conditions that underpin high quality teaching'. While Gunn and Fisk (2013: 47) expand on this by arguing that the nature of teaching awards means that teaching excellence is often retrofitted to winning individuals and enterprises, which then come to be identified as excellent, rather than meeting the requirements of a more strategically defined or understood idea of teaching excellence.

What is demonstrated clearly by teaching excellence awards is that individual excellence has primarily been defined by initiatives and individuals which have come to be recognised as excellent, rather than as having been identified through theoretically robust, systematic or strategic models . . .

For Tsui (2015: 4), it can be the actual award itself that becomes the object of excellence, not the teaching practice: '[i]n some of the modalities, it seems that it is the prestige of the award, rather than what is being awarded, that implies a high level of excellence ... '.

Although we might take a critical view of teaching awards it should not preclude us from appreciating the good practice, hard work from colleagues and genuine student benefit which may have led to the award.

- Teaching award schemes serve a function in highlighting teaching and learning within institutions and across the sector.
- They can create a focus for celebrating achievement and act as a stimulus for colleagues to develop their teaching.
- The strongest and most valid schemes are those with a clear triangulation of views on whether excellence is being demonstrated, beyond simple criteria, where views of peers, students or formal referees are sought to support and validate the claims that are being made in the nomination.

Nonetheless, teaching awards also point to the idea that the excellence within the teaching experience sits more with the individual than the practice. Sharing excellent practice beyond 'show and tell' talks from award winners that is genuinely transferable and provides ideas that can be taken up effectively within other areas can be challenging.

Review point 10.2
TEACHING AWARDS

- What opportunities are there for you to engage with teaching award schemes in your institution?
- How do you think engaging with such a scheme might help you to develop your teaching?
- Think more widely about the opportunities for networking, further scholarly work and perhaps promotion possibilities in addition to the recognition conferred by the award itself.

A LENS ON TEACHING EXCELLENCE

We have seen from examining the three questions posed at the beginning of this chapter on the nature of excellence, the locus of excellence, and whether excellent practice can be shared, that excellence in teaching:

- is a contested concept
- is a global focus for measurement and rankings
- is essentially relational
- needs to be confirmed beyond just meeting criteria by a triangulation of perspectives
- and as a result of being a contextual and situated concept may not be easily transferable across areas of practice.

It may be useful to consider our discussions around excellence through the view of a different lens, part of the approach that we began to explore in Chapter 5, to examine our practice and its development. In the following think piece, Helen King shares with us her thoughts on *expertise* in contrast to excellence, through the lens of Deliberate Practice. Her research in this area involves empirical exploration of the characteristics of expertise in teaching in higher education and a consideration of how this might further inform conversations on excellence.

DELIBERATE PRACTICE – AN ACCESSIBLE ROUTE TO EXCELLENCE?

For a number of years I have been interested in 'ways of thinking and practising' in the disciplines. This has included exploring threshold concepts (Meyer and Land, 2003), signature pedagogies (Gurung, Chick and Haynie, 2008), decoding the disciplines (Pace and Middendorf, 2004) and, more recently, the characteristics of expertise in different fields (Ericsson, Charness, Feltovich and Hoffman, Eds., 2006). As someone who works with academics to develop their teaching, I am particularly interested in supporting colleagues to improve and enhance their practice. This has led me to ask what might be the ways of thinking and practising and, hence, the characteristics of expertise in teaching in HE? The trouble with excellence is that, by definition and derivation, it is not achievable by everyone. Excellence is about being outstanding i.e. standing out from others. From an individual teacher's perspective, this isn't necessarily very motivational. Excellence might be seen as unachievable or not worth aiming for if it's an accolade only available to a limited few. In contrast, the literature on 'expertise' offers a potentially more accessible perspective which can be achieved by all who wish to do so.

Expertise has been explored in a broad range of fields and the literature reveals a number of common characteristics (Bransford, Brown and Cocking, 2000). One particular feature of expertise is the way in which it is developed, improved and maintained. One model identifies this as a dynamic, self-determined process known as Deliberate Practice (Ericsson, Krampe and Tesch-Romer, 1993). Deliberate Practice has four key elements – time, focus, feedback and motivation – and is perhaps most easily illustrated through my example from music. I have been playing the piano since I was about 4 years old (over 40 years ago), I had lessons until I was 18, achieved Grade 8 (the highest exam grade offered by the Associated Board of the Royal Schools of Music) and then continued playing for pleasure. I have had a lot of 'time on task' and have achieved an appropriate level of competency that suits me. But I am not an expert; I am by no means a concert pianist. When I practise, I usually just repeat the pieces of music that I know and enjoy playing. If I tackle something new, I will tend to skip over the tricky bits and focus on what I can do. Through this approach I'm maintaining a good level of competency but I'm not improving – and this is fine for me. If I wanted to improve, Deliberate Practice would be the way to do it. Taking the time to focus on those sections that are difficult, getting feedback (listening to myself or getting comments from others) and adjusting accordingly. But I'm happy as I am and don't have the motivation to practise in this way.

So it is with teaching in higher education (and in many other fields – Van de Wiel, 2004). Some teachers have reached a satisfactory level of competency and continue to rehearse their standard approach, and for many this works fine. In some cases, this level of competency has ceased to achieve the same results over time and student feedback becomes more negative. A colleague taking an expertise approach would consider this feedback, focus on the areas for development and try again – expertise isn't about being good all the time, it's an ongoing process of enhancement. In my experience (as I have observed as part of my support for individuals' professional development), a non-expertise approach would involve using the same teaching materials year after year, tending to blame the students for not engaging, and having little intrinsic motivation to modify their practice.

I have had to demonstrate my approach and commitment to continuing professional development (CPD) as a central aspect of my practice, and it matches closely to the four elements of Deliberate Practice as it needs:

- **Time:** identifying this CPD as an integrated part of my academic work and making the time for it. Also, accepting that it may be some time until the improvements really begin to show.
- **Feedback:** being open to feedback from a variety of sources including self-reflection, and learning from others through observations, conversations, reading the literature, participating in conferences, networks and other networking opportunities.
- **Focus:** drawing on the feedback to identify specific areas for improvement in order to focus my efforts.
- **Motivation:** an element of extrinsic motivation e.g. annual appraisal or review, student evaluations; and lots of intrinsic motivation.

For myself and other experienced colleagues – after participating in often mandatory, formal development opportunities earlier on in our careers – this ongoing process of professional development is self-determined but doesn't have to happen in isolation. The feedback element of Deliberate Practice exposes us to formal and informal communities of practice through which we can discuss, share, problem-solve, critique and improve.

Having explored the concept of Deliberate Practice for some time, I decided to 'practise what I preach' and to apply it to learning a new musical instrument, the banjo. In my experience, the approach really works and I am progressing much more than I would have using my previous complacent methods. Of course, it all seems obvious, but I find that I have gained a lot of intrinsic motivation from knowing that putting in the effort will lead to improvements and that this is backed up by extensive research in a wide range of fields. Indeed, Ericsson (2017) suggests that if the criteria for Deliberate Practice can be defined in a field (any field), then application of that criteria will result in improvements in performance.

So, in conclusion, how might the concept of Deliberate Practice be useful for you?

- Use it as an alternative and complementary approach to reflective practice.
- Employ mechanisms such as peer review, student evaluation, pedagogic research, corridor conversations and chats over

UNDERSTANDING TEACHING EXCELLENCE

coffee, helping others, reading journals, books and magazine, participating in and/or contributing to seminars, conferences, workshops and courses.
- Rather than trying to change everything at once, focus your development activities on those particular areas of need. Regular review will enable you to shift this focus appropriately and, over time, your repertoire of knowledge and skill will broaden and deepen.
- Be reassured that the time and thought investment you make into improving your teaching will pay off in terms of enhancing your confidence and enjoyment in teaching, and improving your students' learning experience.

ASPIRING TO EXCELLENCE IN TEACHING AND LEARNING

What vehicles can you use to aspire to excellence; essentially, to enhance your practice in supporting the development of excellent student learning? Reading this book is a good start! But are there models, approaches, paths that one can follow? Adopting a different perspective on the concept of teaching excellence, such as the 'deliberate practice' approach outlined above by Helen King, is something you can try. Aligning your practice with a developmental framework such as the UKPSF, or a similar structure from your own disciplinary area, can also help you to frame excellence in order to better understand what it looks like in your context. Routes to excellence can also be found in places and from sources other than just ourselves. In this case study, Eilidh Cage from Royal Holloway, University of London, discusses the role that *her students* have played in supporting her attainment of excellence.

Case study 10.2
DEVELOPING EXCELLENCE TOGETHER

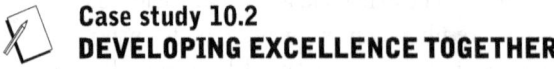
Eilidh Cage, Royal Holloway, University of London

At my university, the number of students registered with our Disability Services for mental health conditions has doubled since 2015; and we are not alone in experiencing this increase. Statistics from the Higher Education

Statistics Authority (HESA) indicate that a high proportion of students report mental health difficulties, and that many students drop out of university due to these difficulties. It is also likely that there are many students who experience mental health issues but do not report this to their university. Ultimately, experiences of mental health difficulties while at university impact on student experience.

Concerned by the statistics and through encountering many anxious, depressed and distressed students in my role as personal tutor, I decided to conduct a research project examining mental health at university. Importantly, I wanted the research project to have students at its centre – after all, they are the ones who know their own experiences best. I therefore used a participatory research approach, working together with four final year psychology undergraduates to develop the research project.

The project was outside of the students' degree programme, with the four students working with me as co-researchers. The four students all had a connection to the topic of mental health and were all extremely passionate about improving mental health at university. The students set the agenda for the research, and rather than a supervisor or lead researcher, I acted as a mentor and facilitator, helping to guide the students in their research, and not imposing my own agenda onto the project. Nonetheless I also served to share my knowledge with the students, as a researcher and teacher, and to quality assure the project.

- In the initial stages of the research, I facilitated discussions trying to identify the issues facing students in relation to mental health.
- We reflected on our own experiences and developed a consensus on some of the key issues.
- We then identified that the aim of our project would be to look at the barriers to accessing mental health support at university.
- We brainstormed some of the possible barriers and designed our project together, putting together a survey and disseminating it widely.
- Almost 300 people were recruited to complete the survey, testament to the students' communication skills and dedication to the project.
- We ultimately plan to publish the findings of our research.

Through working with me as researchers, the students were taught how to hone their research skills and develop self-efficacy in research. Crucially, by working together and creating a warm, supportive atmosphere, the students learned about leading research, instead of acting as assistants to research or feeling that they were just helping me out with my research. By working together, I believe that I have been able to show excellence in my teaching *because of them*. Partnering together, developing our ideas and listening to their experiences has made me a better researcher and teacher. Treating students as equals, especially when it comes to topics that concern them, serves to benefit everyone involved.

Developing excellence can also come as a result of a more collaborative approach to practice. One of the reasons that teaching awards can feel uncomfortable is that they often focus on the individual, when in reality much of what we do as professionals in higher education involves working with others, whether that's developing a new curriculum, team teaching, leading a module team, or collaborating on a development project. Look around for team teaching awards, such as the Advance HE Collaborative Award for Teaching Excellence (CATE) which 'recognises and rewards collaborative work that has had a demonstrable impact on teaching and learning' that you can enter with colleagues to acknowledge your collaborative practice. In the following case study, John Bostock describes how a collegiate approach supports excellence in teaching for learning at Edge Hill University

Case study 10.3
CULTURAL GLUE

John Bostock, Edge Hill University

For over a decade, Edge Hill University has operated a university Teaching and Learning Fellowship which, since 2012, I have formally led. Initially an opportunity to research and showcase best practice based on an individual's research, it has evolved into something much more intricate and complex. The Fellowship is, in effect, a network of 52 colleagues who work in various roles in academic and service areas and who promote and champion teaching and learning excellence.

The overarching priority for the Fellowship is to support colleagues who in turn influence students' development of their intellectual, practical and creative potential. In practice, the Fellowship is designed to positively:

- enhance student learning by the dissemination of good practice across the university
- recognise and support excellence in teaching for learning and learning support activity

- strengthen the implementation of the University Teaching and Learning Strategy.

The Fellowship scheme has increased engagement across the university in dialogue around teaching and learning and has placed renewed emphasis on the Fellowship's developmental aspects. This is realised in the three ways main activities of Fellows, as outlined in Figure 10.2.

The approach taken in the scheme means that Fellows are instrumental in supporting three distinct yet interconnected University mechanisms for maintaining quality teaching and learning.

The Fellowship scheme provides a vehicle for colleagues to achieve personal and professional development; contribute to a vibrant community of

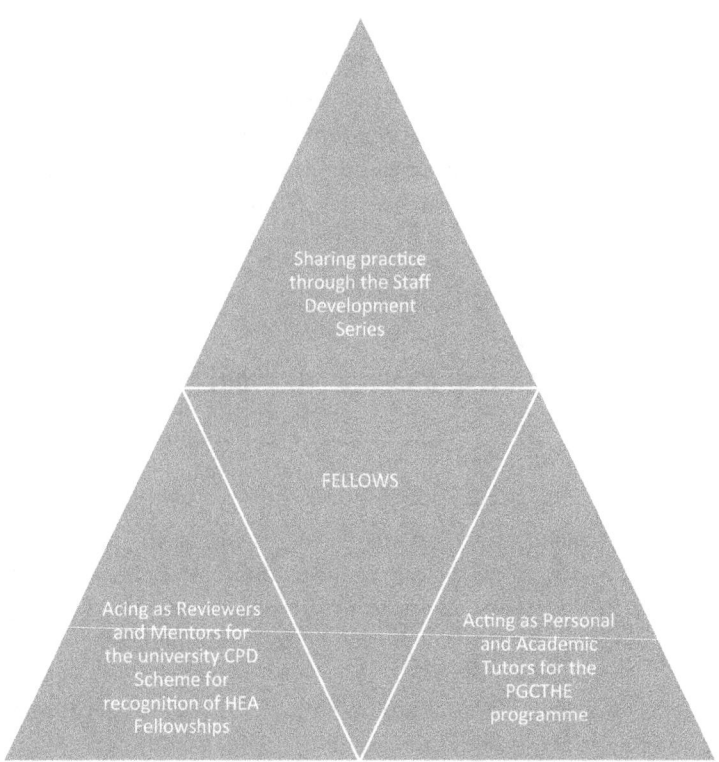

FIGURE 10.2. Triangulation of perspectives on developing excellence through Teaching and Learning Fellowships

student learning by sharing practical examples that work; and to excel through this activity. Described as institutional and cultural glue, it is a Fellowship that operates on collegiality and intrinsic passion, supporting excellence in teaching at Edge Hill.

When presented in this way, striving for excellence becomes something that can become a unifying force.

In order to better understand teaching excellence within an enhancement-led culture, we need to re-frame our thinking around excellence, moving away from a focus on the traits of the *individual* teacher or even the central aspects of their practice, and to look instead at the experience of the learners. One needs to have a belief in one's practice as a way to achieve excellent learning outcomes for our students. For Skelton (2009: 109) this 'can only follow from a serious commitment to the reflexive development of a value-laden and morally defensible practice'. This is nicely captured in the final case study in this chapter where Maria Godinho shares an experience from her practice as a new teacher in higher education and how her reflections on this early experience helped consolidate her understanding of what excellent teaching can look like.

Case study 10.4
'EDUCATION CAN CHANGE THE WORLD'

Maria Godinho, University of Edinburgh

My formal training as a teacher started with a Postgraduate Teaching Internship, then offered at the University of Western Australia where I was completing my PhD in neuroscience. As part of my teaching plan during the internship I gave a lecture called Careers in Science to second year undergraduate students; I remembered that when I was an undergraduate student in Biology at the University of Evora, in Portugal, I wasn't quite sure what would I be doing in my future career as a scientist.

In preparation for the lecture I consulted an experienced professor in my School who shared her notes on a similar session she ran for her Honour students. I also visited Student Services for advice on job searching and their thoughts on the transferable skills students should keep in mind, so that during the remaining time at university they could prepare themselves for their future careers. I included information about career progression in academia as well as suggestions of jobs outside academia where the skills they were learning would be valued.

The lecture went well. A few months later I saw a student from that course, and asked him how he was doing. He told me that actually, following my lecture, he had decided to change his degree. For a while he had been wondering whether or not a science degree was really what he wanted to pursue, as he wasn't particularly excited with what he was learning. After my lecture he made the decision that science was not what he would like to be doing in the future and so changed to another degree. He was finding his new course really interesting and was really happy with his new career path.

I was so excited! I had always thought that 'education can change the world' and here was a real life example of someone making a change to their life partly because of something they were exposed to in one of my lectures. In my over-enthusiasm I couldn't help but share this story with a senior colleague who I greatly admired. To my surprise she commented on this as being a big failure: I should be enticing students to study science and instead, my lecture had put this student off and he chose to study something else.

When this conversation happened I was still very much an early career teacher. In the last decade since then I have often reflected on this episode. My opinion of it all now is that the lecture about careers in science and the subsequent conversation with the student was one of the most rewarding moments of my career as a teacher. Rather than a teacher pushing their own particular agenda they should share in the joy of their students' satisfaction and fulfilment. It reaffirmed my conviction that an excellent teacher is one who enables students to realise their potential and to be happier as a result.

CONCLUSIONS

Understandings of excellence can be found in many different places, can have diverse owners and can have been arrived at through a variety of routes. We have seen how this contributes to the challenges around the concept of excellence. Wood and Su (2017: 462) comment on the need for 'the development of a shared "currency" in terms of understandings of teaching excellence and that this should also include understandings of student learning in higher education.' We would agree; and encourage you to reflect on the primary objective of teaching excellence being its demonstration through excellence in learning. Beyond the contention over definitions, measurements and metrics, and institutional rankings, the most important part of understanding teaching excellence is to own it personally and to make it live within your practice to the benefit of your students' learning. As we saw in Chapter 5, development comes through a critically reflective approach to practice; not necessarily through years at the 'chalk face'. Excellence is therefore attainable for you at any stage of your career.

- Think about taking a different approach to understanding excellence – what might that look like in your practice?
- Who might you collaborate with in developing teaching excellence – your peers, your students, or perhaps a whole department approach?
- How can you encourage your colleagues and your students to explore the concept of teaching excellence with you?

 REFERENCES

Benner, P. (1984). *From Novice to Expert: Excellence and Power in Clinical Nursing Practice*. CA: Addison-Wesley.

Bransford, J. D., Brown, A. L. & Cocking, R. R. (eds.) (2000). *How People Learn: Brain, Mind, Experience, and School*. Washington, DC: The National Academies Press.

Dreyfus, H. L. & Dreyfus, S. E. (1986). *Mind over Machine. The Power of Human Intuition and Expertise in the Era of the Computer*. Oxford: Basil Blackwell.

Eraut, M. (1994). *Developing Professional Knowledge and Competence*. London: Falmer Press.

Ericsson, K. A. (2017). Expertise and individual differences: The search for the structure and acquisition of experts' superior performance. *WIREs Cogn Sci, 8*.

Ericsson, K. A., Charness, N., Feltovich, P. J. & Hoffman, R. R. (Eds.) (2006). *The Cambridge Handbook of Expertise and Expert Performance*. New York: Cambridge University Press.

Ericsson, K. A., Krampe, R. Th. & Tesch-Romer, C. (1993). The role of Deliberate Practice in the acquisition of expert performance. *Psychological Review, 100*(3), 363–406.

Gunn, V. & Fisk, A. (2013). *Considering Teaching Excellence in Higher Education: 2007 – 2013*. York: Higher Education Academy. www.heacademy.ac.uk/sites/default/files/resources/TELR_final_acknowledgements.pdf [Online, accessed 16 September, 2018]

Gurung, R. A. R., Chick, N. L. & Haynie, A. (2008). *Exploring Signature Pedagogies: Approaches to Teaching Disciplinary Habits of Mind*. Sterling. VA: Stylus Publishing.

Land, R. & Gordon, G. (2015). *Teaching Excellence Initiatives: Modalities and Operational Factors*. Higher Education Academy.

Little, B., Locke, W., Parker, J. & Richardson, J. (2007). *Excellence in Teaching and Learning. A Review of the Literature for the Higher Education Academy*. Centre for Higher Education Research and Information, The Open University. www.heacademy.ac.uk/system/files/litreview_excellence_in_tl_cheri_jul07.pdf [Online, accessed 16 September 2018]

Meyer, J. H. F. & Land, R. (2003). Threshold concepts and troublesome knowledge 1 – Linkages to ways of thinking and Practising. In C. Rust (ed.), *Improving Student Learning – Ten Years On*. Oxford: OCSLD.

Pace, D. & Middendorf, J. (Eds.) (2004). Decoding the disciplines: Helping students learn disciplinary ways of thinking. *New Directions for Teaching and Learning*, No. 98.

Saunders, D. & Blanco Ramirez, G. (2017). Against 'teaching excellence': Ideology, commodification, and enabling the neoliberalization of postsecondary education. *Teaching in Higher Education*, 22(4), 396–407.

Skelton, A. (2005). *Understanding Teaching Excellence in Higher Education: Towards a Critical Approach*. Abingdon: Routledge.

Skelton, A. (2009). A 'teaching excellence' for the times we live in? *Teaching in Higher Education*, 14(1), 107 – 12.

Su, F. & Wood, M. (2012). What makes a good university lecturer? Students' perceptions of teaching excellence. *Journal of Applied Research in Higher Education*, 4(2), 142 – 55.

Tsui, A. B. M. (2015). A critical commentary on Ray Land and George Gordon 'Teaching excellence initiatives: Modalities and operational factors'. Higher Education Academy.

Van de Wiel, M., Szegedi, K. H. P. & Weggeman, M. C. D. P. (2004). Professional learning: Deliberate attempts at developing expertise. In H. P. A. Boshuizen, R. Bromme & H. Gruber (eds.), *Professional Learning: Gaps and Transitions on the Way from Novice to Expert*. Dordrecht: Kluwer Academic Publishers.

Wood, M. & Su, F. (2017). What makes an excellent lecturer? Academics' perspectives on the discourse of 'teaching excellence' in higher education. *Teaching in Higher Education*, 22(4), 451 – 66.

Chapter 11

Career-wide enhancement

INTRODUCTION

The idea of complexity – or even super-complexity (Barnett, 2000) – as a backdrop for all our activities, including learning, working and thriving, is one that has become all pervasive. Where once the career directions and opportunities for enhancement for teachers and researchers working in higher education were clear – perhaps even fixed – that is no longer the case. Universities operate within a business mindset to a much greater extent than they did in previous years. Competition is fuelled by rising student fees, the race to secure the overseas market, and an increased focus on growing areas of practice that can meet the demands of that market, such as business, enterprise and entrepreneurship. Academic freedom can feel under pressure and academics themselves can feel similarly squeezed out of their comfort zones – and in some cases their discipline areas when research funding dries up or institutional priorities change – and into ways of working that they would not have envisaged as being part of their career path, five or ten years ago.

Yet, any kind of disruption has the potential to create new opportunities. Rather than focusing on what's no longer open to you or the skills and knowledge that you don't have in order to develop in your current career path, take advantage of the situation. Re-visit the models of development that we outlined in Chapter 1 and move on from a deficit way of thinking and adopt instead an enhancement-based approach. Such an approach involves taking 'deliberate steps' (QAA, 2017: 3) to reflect upon and improve your practice, and can be a good way to surface new opportunities and possibilities. This chapter looks at how you might take an enhancement-based approach in the context of your career development; the range of opportunities to achieve this that might be available to you and how you might take those forward; and also how you might take a step or two further to stretch your potential. We've also included a CPD planner at the end of the chapter to help you reflect on your progress as you take an enhancement-based approach to developing your teaching across your career.

TAKING AN ENHANCEMENT-LED APPROACH TO CAREER-WIDE LEARNING

The Future of Learning: Preparing for Change (Redecker, Leis, Leendertse, Punie, Gijsbers, Kirschner, Stoyanov and Hoogveld, 2011) – an EU Commission report – forecast that the central paradigm of future learning will be characterised by life-long and life-wide learning, shaped by the all-pervasiveness of what we would now call online technologies and digital literacies. We will all need a little more time, and for us all to get a little bit older, before we can testify personally with regard to life-*long* learning. However, life-*wide* learning is something that is for the here and now. Jackson (n.d.: 9) describes it as follows:

> all learning and personal development that emerges through activities in the multiple contexts and situations we inhabit contemporaneously at any point in our life, with the aim of fulfilling roles and achieving specific goals, and continuously developing knowledge, understanding, skills, capabilities, dispositions and values within personal, civic, social and/or employment-related contexts.

Ron Barnett (in Jackson, n.d.: 13) provides a philosophical perspective on life-wide learning: 'A philosophy of perpetual becoming driven by purpose and intent of pursuing personal growth and realising our own potential . . . in which we have responsibility to author our lives'.

In this chapter, we take Jackson's ideas and Barnett's perspectives on life-wide learning and apply them specifically to enhancing your teaching, as part of a career-wide approach to development.

What you have to do versus what you want to do

The idea of a Postgraduate Certificate, or PG Cert, in teaching and learning or academic practice in higher education is now a commonplace form of continuing professional development (CPD) for university teachers. In the majority of UK HEIs, completing part or all of this kind of qualification is a requirement for probationary lecturers. More than simply an accepted part of CPD they are now embraced as an important aspect of professionalisation of the role of university teacher. The pros and cons and drivers for this approach to developing your teaching are discussed elsewhere in this book but as has been seen, it can influence personal attitudes towards engaging in CPD.

While PG Certs were in the vanguard of mandatory development for academics, the idea of mandatory 'training' – for all staff – has become a much wider movement. Areas such as equality and diversity, data protection and cyber-security are all commonly delivered as online training, and represent CPD on an institution-wide scale aimed at mass engagement and universal compliance. While providing a convenient and effective vehicle for the delivery of important information, largely driven by legislative requirements, it is often presented as a 'tick box and move on' approach to CPD. So how can you get the most of out of any mandatory training that you are required to do, at any stage of your career?

Begin by viewing the training course in a positive light! It's part of human nature to react negatively to being told that we 'have' to do anything – and it can be particularly galling if you feel you already have a particular knowledge or experience in one of these areas. Let's think about it differently.

- The mandatory training on offer at your institution will constitute high-quality, state-of-the-art professional development – that's also free!
- Approach the course by adopting a *learning* rather than *target completion* mindset.

Online courses of this nature tend to be quite content rich and are peppered with key facts and information that you will be required to remember, and then to demonstrate that you have remembered, through multiple choice questions that are usually presented at the end of each section. The better courses provide guidance on where you went wrong if you answer a question incorrectly, and the best will also provide an explanation of why you got an answer right – aiming to imbue guesswork with some value. These kinds of courses work on a model where a target completion is presented, normally as a percentage of the questions to be answered correctly, before you can be deemed to have successfully undertaken the training. There will also be an institutional target for staff completions in each academic year which provides extra pressure in a time-poor environment.

The temptation to click through the course and literally tick the box-(es) in order to complete it as quickly as possible is understandable. This may well be an efficient approach but it is unlikely to be effective in terms of your individual learning of the course material and its application to practice in the longer term. Here are some suggestions to get the most of out of the experience.

- Keep a notebook with you while you work through the online course and make notes! This may seem obvious but while course content may remain available to you after you've completed the course it may not be easy to find.
- Think about working with a colleague or group of colleagues to complete the training. While each of you will be required to complete it individually, you can get more value out of sitting together and discussing the questions while you complete it individually online. You can bring even more value to the discussion by relating the topics and questions to real life examples from your practice.
- Ask whether there are any workshops or discussion sessions provided alongside the online content. If there aren't any, consider setting up something yourself.
- Compile a list of all of the mandatory training that you are required to do and identify when the best time will be for you to engage with it, within the timescale allowed.

You'll see that many of these suggestions reflect the kinds of things that you would normally say to your own students – so make sure that you follow your own advice. Now that you have completed the course you can get the credit for it by downloading your digital certificate of completion. Or perhaps your institution has an open badge scheme aligned with mandatory training, so you can receive your 'badge'. But why bother? Doesn't this all feel a bit childish, like being back in the Guides or Scouts? Getting into good habits with respect to recording your CPD activities is a useful thing to do and may in fact be required by your institution. Maintaining any associated certificates provides a validated date stamp of your activity. You will need somewhere to store digital certificates but remember to think carefully about the platform you use for this purpose. Your institution's VLE or e-portfolio might be convenient but you will probably not be able to take the contents with you if you move institution. Look for a solution that it is transferable.

Review point 11.1
GETTING THE MOST OUT OF MANDATORY TRAINING

Always think about 'where next?' as a result of this kind of training. How might you adapt your teaching in light of what you have learned? What can you take from a course on cyber-security that could inform your teaching and your students' learning? How could that learning be shared more widely within your department, school or faculty?

PG CERT PLUS

What next after your PG Cert in teaching and learning or academic practice? Where can you go now with your professional development? Some colleagues view completion of their PG Cert as 'job done'. We're back in that tick box mentality – but that's not where you want to be. Effective engagement with your studies should be opening doors and highlighting areas that you want to explore further, not closing them down. This could be through the connections and contacts you've made with your peer learners or as a result of a teaching-related project you undertook as part of your studies. Or it could be through learning about a pedagogical approach that is new to your discipline area or gaining confidence in a new teaching approach that you would like to try with your students. As we discussed in Chapter 8, investigating or researching your own practice in this way supports your commitment to your career as a university teacher.

Your PG Cert should be the start rather than the end point of your development journey if you are a new lecturer, and if you're a more experienced teacher, can also provide opportunities to expand your experience at any career stage. This could be through contributing to the PG Cert curriculum in some way, as opposed to engaging with the programme yourself, perhaps through contributing case studies or getting involved as a peer reviewer. Being a successful learner is an iterative process and involves re-visiting and re-evaluating one's understanding of previous learning and experiences – at whatever age or stage.

Figuring out where to go next can be challenging. Should it be further courses of study or something from that interesting workshop programme? Credit bearing or informal? How should you decide? What will be of most benefit to your practice – and potentially to your promotion prospects? How can you make the time to engage in all of this ongoing development? The only one of these questions that we can answer for you with any certainty is the last one; and the answer is that it is definitely possible, and indeed essential, to do so. Nonetheless, it is something that is difficult to do on your own, so you will need to call on support to help you with this. How so? There will be a range of support options available to you, not all of which might be immediately obvious, so start local.

Speak to your line manager. As the person responsible for allocating and managing your workload, this conversation should be top of your list. Work by Eraut and Hirsh (2007) concluded that the four top level influencers of effective (and hindrances to) workplace learning are: individual-level factors, team-level factors, the approach to learning and development, and line management. Staff development sessions are strewn with the empty chairs of colleagues who wanted to attend the workshop but were unable to prioritise the event in their workload. The result is disappointment and frustration as well as lost opportunity. Who knows how many new colleagues you could have added to your network, or if you might have been able to get some advice on how to address that concerning issue with your first year tutorial group, or if you could have shared your ideas for a teaching project with a potential collaborator; and that's all before you get to what the actual workshop was about.

- 'Manage your manager' by bringing to their attention the kinds of development activities that you would like to pursue and highlighting the potential impact that they could have on your practice.
- Align your aspirations with local and institutional aims and objectives.
- Demonstrate how engagement in these activities would address your personal objectives, set through probation or annual review.
- Be prepared to argue the case for bringing added value to the department, school or faculty through these activities.
- Ask your line manager's advice and be prepared to listen; they have the benefit of being able to see the 'bigger picture' and to help you to successfully fit into it.
- Does your institution have a staff development or CPD policy? These can sometimes be hard to find but mainly tend to sit on Human Resources or Organisational Development websites.

These policies provide an insight into your university's perspective on staff CPD. You should be able to find here information with regard to any institutional *expectations* on you to engage with CPD or annual *allocation* of time for staff to engage in CPD.

Discuss with your mentor. Depending on your career stage you may have a probationary, PG Cert or research mentor or you may be involved in a coaching programme. All of these schemes are well placed to support you in exploring your ideas and helping you to clarify your aims and aspirations. Mentoring relationships facilitate personal and professional development through support, challenge and review and have real potential to help us in developing our teaching, as the primary focus of the activity is on learning and growth. Working with a formal or informal mentor and growing your network of supportive colleagues makes for a very positive workplace in which to experiment with and develop your teaching practice. There is little more deflating than a work environment where the ethos of 'that's the way we've always done things around here' holds sway, accompanied by a pressure not to rock the boat with new ideas and approaches. While supported learning is an excellent way to enable you to develop your teaching, nonetheless, unremitting support is of less value than support with challenge. This is where your mentor will help you in critiquing and illuminating issues and proposals, before supporting you in their implementation by carrying out the role of a critical friend. This process provides a continuous cycle of supported and critical evaluation which can lead to enhanced practice. The following case study from one of us demonstrates the impact that can be realised through a good mentoring relationship.

Case study 11.1
MY FIRST MENTOR

I changed horses mid-race, if you like, moving from one discipline to another as one career door closed and another opened. It was exciting moving into a new area but also very challenging. At times the learning curve was so steep it felt as if it were vertical. It was a new world, with a more senior role, and a new 'language'. However, I was really fortunate in that one of my new colleagues was incredibly supportive and encouraging. She helped me to find my feet and my confidence in the new area. What did she do that was so helpful? It's hard to put into words really. She was supportive, encouraging, and never patronising. We talked a lot – about all sorts of things. We planned teaching sessions together, she gave me ideas and also helped me to think about my own. She played a number of roles – supporting me but also quietly questioning some of my more strident views, challenging them, and getting me to look at them more critically. I wanted to have her vision and foresight and she became my role model for developing as a teacher in my new discipline. We have also become good friends but we still have that ability to step outside ourselves and to become more objective and evaluate what the other is doing. I suppose, although I didn't think about this until later, that she was my first mentor. It was extremely valuable for me and I owe her a lot.

You might also like to consider extending the value of these kinds of relationships by working with an action learning set. These are essentially groups of critical friends who meet together to discuss and consider a particular issue or concern. At each meeting one individual has the chance to have their issue examined and discussed in detail within the action learning set. As with mentoring, the role of the set is not to immediately offer advice and to tell the individual what they should do, but rather it is to explore the issue in greater depth by open questioning, providing support and challenge throughout, and by allowing the individual concerned to arrive at their own, informed, decisions. Essentially, the action learning set is a form of group mentoring. We looked at an example of an action learning set in one of the case studies in Chapter 6, where we considered collective practice. You might want to revisit that case study in light of this discussion.

Utilise relevant frameworks. One way to approach planning your ongoing CPD is to identify a framework against which you can map your development. Generic frameworks include the UK Professional Standards Framework (UKPSF) and the VITAE Researcher Development Framework (RDF) while many professions also have their own discipline-related frameworks, such as the Association of Medical Educators (AoME). The top level elements of these three frameworks are outlined in Table 11.1.

Frameworks such as these can be helpful in supporting self-evaluation, identification of gaps in your personal skill set and identifying directions in which you would like to develop. As discussed in Chapter 7, looking at drivers in HE, there are many and various reasons behind the creation and proliferation of these frameworks. As a result there is a certain amount of stamping of authority and ownership over academic identities that goes on, including a pigeon-holing of the qualities and attributes of the associated identity. Don't limit yourself! Frameworks can provide a helpful tool to explore attributes but they are necessarily compact by design and limited

TABLE 11.1 Examples of frameworks to support practice development

Framework	Description	Aim	Expression
UKPSF	A comprehensive set of professional standards and guidelines for everyone involved in teaching and supporting learning in higher education (HE), aimed at individual and institutional levels.	The framework identifies the diverse range of teaching and support roles and environments in HE. These are reflected and expressed in the Dimensions of Professional Practice within HE teaching and learning support which map with Fellowship descriptors.	The Dimensions of Professional Practice: ■ activity undertaken by teachers and support staff ■ core knowledge needed to carry out those activities at the appropriate level ■ professional values that individuals performing these activities should exemplify.
RDF	Sets out wide-ranging knowledge, intellectual abilities, techniques and professional standards for individuals expected to do research, as well as the personal qualities, knowledge and skills to work with others and ensure the wider impact of research.	The framework is structured into four domains covering the knowledge, behaviours and attributes of researchers. Within each of the domains there are three sub-domains and associated descriptors.	The 4 domains: ■ knowledge and intellectual abilities ■ personal effectiveness ■ research governance and organisation ■ engagement, influence and impact

CAREER-WIDE ENHANCEMENT

Framework	Description	Aim	Expression
AoME	Professional standards framework and qualification systems aligned with research for the continuing development of professional medical education; and the promotion and dissemination of current best practice in medical education.	Set of core values and five key practice domains. Each domain contains detailed descriptions of elements, outlining the expected understanding, skills and capabilities. These detailed outcomes describe and underpin expert professional practice in medical education. Each element is sub-divided into three levels.	The domains are: ■ designing and planning learning ■ teaching and facilitating learning ■ assessment of learning ■ educational research and scholarship ■ educational management and leadership

in the depth in which they can articulate or explore issues and ideas. Ways to get round these limitations include cross referencing frameworks that are relevant to your practice and the use of lenses to interrogate your practice. One example is provided in the RDF where it notes that lenses such as employability and enterprise can be used to look 'at professional development . . . [in order to] help researchers strengthen their academic profile or prepare for transition into a new area of work' and the Advance HE guidance on how a digital lens can be used to engage with the UKPSF.

TAKING ADVANTAGE OF OPPORTUNITIES AND GOING WIDE

One of the challenges of taking a career-wide perspective can be the large number of possibilities provided by such a wide range of opportunities all at once, rather than the more linear approach where 'xyz' follow one after the other. The 'xyz' approach to career development is often time-bound and restrictive. It is inextricably linked with sectoral, institutional, peer, perhaps societal and often economic expectations about progression in relation to age, experience, gender, available resource, and established norms. As we saw in Chapter 7, these kinds of drivers can provide barriers as well as opportunities. Taking a career-wide approach, and looking around you rather than always upwards can provide interest and opportunities that you might not have anticipated; which may in turn lead to developing expertise and career advancement.

- Take part in a conference that is allied to but slightly outside of your immediate field of interest. How might this different 'take' on your own area of practice yield benefits? What new contacts can you make? What kinds of opportunities exist for collaboration?

Even better . . . organise your own multi-disciplinary workshop, symposium or conference and develop associated skills in events management.

- Work with your Students' Association to genuinely see things from a student-centred perspective. Do they have a campaign, such as a focus on assessment and feedback or engaging PG students that you could support? How can this experience help to inform your teaching? How might it influence your thinking about partnership working with students that we discussed in Chapter 4?

Even better . . . make it your mission to ensure that student-staff committees or feedback mechanisms are working effectively in your department, school or faculty and then across the wider institution. Are there guidelines and good practice that can be developed and shared? What's the experience in other universities? Organise an event for staff and students from your local institutions to share practice.

- Learn a new skill, perhaps in relation to a piece of technology to support learning such as lecture capture or effective use of social media tools for teaching and learning. Or go back to basics and really learn how to use tools such as Word or Excel *properly* (you'll be amazed by the functionality that has always been there but you've not made the time to learn).

Even better . . . use your learning from this activity to develop guidelines and easy to use checklists to support colleagues in creating fully accessible documents and teaching materials. Not only will this provide materials that can be accessed immediately by students with disabilities – who are using text to speech readers for example – but it will also produce high quality materials that are easier to update and provide a good learning experience for all students.

 Review point 11.2
GOING WIDE

Think about developing your capabilities within your current role. What can your current level of expertise be used for that will in turn help you to develop further in that area? Look around for opportunities to be:

- an external examiner
- a Summer School tutor
- a peer reviewer
- a member on a teaching awards panel

Or think about:

- engaging with local or institutional change initiatives
- becoming a mentor
- growing your profile as a leader in teaching by applying for Senior Fellow (SFHEA) or Principal Fellow (PFHEA) of the Higher Education Academy, as appropriate
- offering to provide master classes, or a guest lecture, or to develop a podcast to contribute to other colleagues' courses in your particular area of expertise.

Or if you would really like to challenge and stretch yourself, how about becoming a TEDx speaker. TEDx talks are held world-wide with the aim of sparking 'conversation and connection through TED experiences at the local level' around 'ideas worth spreading'. Take a proactive approach by:

- doing your research – visit the TEDx events page to see what's coming up
- check the application process for your local talks – is it an open call or do they need a proposal?

- make sure that what you would like to talk about fits with the theme of the event
- increase your visibility – blog, tweet, create a buzz
- understand the nature of the TEDx talk – don't waste the opportunity by hitting the wrong note!

(adapted from Clark, 2014)

If you live in the UK, Ireland or Australia, how about discovering your inner comic? Train and participate in Bright Club, 'the platform that transforms researchers into stand-up comedians' in order to stretch your potential, hone your presentation skills and develop confidence; in addition to letting your colleagues see you in a whole new light. Lectures will hold no fears for you ever again after you've had a gig as a stand-up!

There are also many activities to share practice or develop and use your expertise that you can undertake without ever leaving your desk but which can have a global impact.

- Develop materials under a Creative Commons licence and see your work grow and flourish as others add their thoughts to it.
- Author a Wikipedia page in your area of expertise or special interest.
- Take on a role as a reviewer or a translator for an educational body such as the Khan Academy.
- Create your own blog, website or YouTube channel.

Opportunities for sharing practice can be local, national or international and either face-to-face, in print or online. They can take the form of academic papers, interactive workshops or blog posts. They can provide vehicles for the dissemination of evidence-informed practice or discussion of blue-skies thinking. They have the potential to stimulate discussion or stifled yawns – and maybe even the odd raised eyebrow. In whatever shape they take there have never been more platforms available to get your ideas out there. But why restrict yourself to this side of the equation? What opportunities might there be to get involved in reviewing conference proposals or journal articles? Or in organising an event or publishing its proceedings? Getting involved in this kind of activity can provide many benefits to your personal and professional development as described in the following case study by Jane Pritchard from the University of Bristol.

Case study 11.2
WE STARTED A JOURNAL (!)

Jane Pritchard, University of Bristol

It's over ten years now since I got together with a couple of colleagues to set up the PESTLHE (Practice and Evidence of Scholarship of Teaching and Learning in Higher Education) online journal. At that time there was a clear gap in terms of accessible journals focusing on teaching and learning in higher education where newer colleagues could find a good home for their experiences and ideas. The journal set out to offer an opportunity for those involved in University learning and teaching to publish accounts of scholarly practice or small-scale practitioner research and case studies, with a focus on enhancement of student learning. More than 26 issues later the journal is still going strong!

Setting up a journal may seem like an ambitious thing to do so why did I decide to get involved? The time seemed right for a number of reasons. Supporting the scholarship of teaching and learning (SoTL) forms a central part of my work as an educational developer and dissemination of practice is a good way to demonstrate SoTL. At that time, there was an increase in the number of colleagues being appointed to Teaching and Scholarship (T&S) contracts, who needed to demonstrate their SoTL activities through sharing their practice; and we were keen to help them find ways to do this. So this provided two clear drivers.

Having like-minded, collegiate and supportive colleagues to work with on the venture was also very important. This included my immediate colleagues in the educational development team but also others from the library and IT department. Everyone played a part in setting up what needed to be a sustainable platform which would be online, no cost and open access. We also needed to ensure the journal's sustainability with a requirement for minimal support and by developing its own branding, rather than having the appearance of an in-house university publication – PESTLHE began life in one university but changed to another when colleagues moved on, so it was important that we future-proofed the journal branding in this way.

All of this activity took me into new areas of practice and helped me to enhance or develop new skill sets. Some of this was personal development. Working as part of a multi-disciplinary team to set up PESTLHE and acting from the outset as the editor-in-chief, my people skills have become finely honed! Setting up and managing a cradle to grave publication system, involving advertising and promotion and encouraging and supporting colleagues to write articles has also made me more pragmatic – and certainly able to more effectively manage several elements of a project simultaneously and with good humour. There have also been benefits for my own professional practice. Working with lots of different authors, writing in a variety of different areas, has improved my knowledge of a wide range of literature whilst reviewing and editing has improved my own writing skills. Virtually meeting so many new colleagues is also great networking, while involvement in PESTLHE has also raised my own profile in the field.

It hasn't been without its challenges of course. Taking on the role of editor-in-chief is a big responsibility and finding time to work on the journal continues to be an issue, working largely on a 'beg, borrow or steal' model! This inevitably restricts the number of issues that go out as the workload has to remain manageable; not least to ensure appropriate support for the authors and to maintain the high quality of the journal. Yet undoubtedly, working on PESTLHE has been hugely fulfilling and has allowed me to play a part in the wider community of sharing practice, turning ideas into good scholarly articles, and it continues to open up new opportunities including linking the journal to local and potentially national workshops on how to write for publication.

Setting up an online journal is definitely possible but:
- look for your niche in order to have the best chance of success for all
- think about testing the water by setting up a blog in your area of interest
- start off by gaining personal experience in reviewing by actively reviewing across a range of journals
- read widely across the learning and teaching journals to develop a good understanding of format and style as well as content to position your own work in the broadest context of HE learning and teaching
- think carefully about the time commitment and workload that setting up a journal will involve
- ensure the right amount of professional support and expertise around you.

CONCLUSIONS

Engaging in any of these different activities will shape how you 'are' as a professional – your identity as teacher and learner and colleague.

Additionally, your profile and reputation will be enhanced and you will have opportunities to grow your career in a number of different directions. A word of caution, however. A developing profile can also place additional demands on our energies and capacity to cope. Creating a Twitter account or blog that generates a lot of interest and followers can be great for networking and sharing ideas; but also creates a lot of expectations and resulting pressure on the tweeter or blogger to produce new and engaging comments or material on a regular basis. While the scope and extent of potential activities can present an exciting prospect initially, it does take effort and commitment to sustain your engagement in the longer term. With so many demands on our time, both professionally and personally, and so many things with which we might engage at any one time we do need to be conscious of potential overload; if not actual burn-out.

Developing coping strategies and building resilience are becoming essential to maintaining good mental health and energy for both ourselves and our students in this information-saturated, super-complex world. A wide range of resilience resources have been developed across the globe, highlighting its nature as a universal concern in contemporary society.

- Australian resource bank: www.unistudentsuccess.com
- The Harvard Resilience Consortium in the US: www.resilienceconsortium.bsc.harvard.edu
- In the UK, AMOSSHE, the Student Services Organisation, has developed this toolkit as a living resource bank, which encourages ongoing contributions: www.resiliencetoolkit.org.uk

Become a good role model in this respect by learning about the skills and strategies behind building resilience for yourself, and then share these approaches with your students.

Your CPD planner

You can use the planner in Table 11.2 at any stage of your career to self-evaluate your development or to generate ideas about 'where next'? Develop it as a living document by adding your own actions, specific to your own learning context.

TABLE 11.2 Your CPD planner

Action	Key learning points	What next?
Keep informed about what is required of you and reflect on how you can go beyond compliance and ensure that learning from these courses can inform your teaching practice. *Mandatory training continues to develop in a number of areas, such as equality & diversity, cyber-security and data protection, and this approach to ensuring compliance and understanding looks set to continue.*		
Explore the opportunities presented by your institutional PG Cert programme at any stage of your career. *Go beyond any probationary requirement and complete your PG Cert – or think about a Masters. Or if you're a more experienced member of staff ask whether you can take any stand-alone modules from the PG Cert as CPD. Or think about contributing to the PG Cert in some way, perhaps as a mentor or by offering a master class in your area.*		
Identify frameworks against which you can map your ongoing development. *Frameworks can help us to take a more structured approach to our practice and to self-evaluate our development. Which works best for you – the generic or the discipline-specific approach? Why is this? What does it tell you about your life-wide learning and development?*		

CAREER-WIDE ENHANCEMENT

Action	Key learning points	What next?
Evidence your achievements for recognition and reward *Capturing, and being able to revisit, reflect upon and review your learning experiences, is an important part of professional practice. Think about using an online portfolio tool, personal blog, or a journal. Which of these fits best with your approach to learning? Which medium makes you want to return to the material and to maintain its usefulness?*		
Consolidate your learning and share practice *Sharing practice that is impactful and can demonstrate real results and genuine learning is a key aspect of scholarly activity. What opportunities exist for you to engage in sharing practice through working with colleagues and presenting or publishing your work?*		
Go wide *Don't restrict yourself to traditional ideas around linear career progression. Explore all avenues. Surprise yourself by trying something that you might have previously discounted. Become a novice again in a new area and enjoy the experience.*		

 REFERENCES

Academy of Medical Educators (2014). *Professional Standards* (3rd edn). Cardiff: Academy of Medical Educators. www.medicaleducators.org/write/MediaManager/AOME_Professional_Standards_2014.pdf [Online, accessed 16 September 2018].

AMOSSHE. www.resiliencetoolkit.org.uk [Online, accessed 16 September 2018].

Australian resource bank. www.unistudentsuccess.com [Online, accessed 16 September 2018].

Barnett, R. (2000). *Realizing the University in an Age of Supercomplexity*. Buckingham: Open University Press.

Bright Club. www.brightclub.org [Online, accessed 16th September 2018].

Clark, D. (2014). How to become a TEDx speaker. www.forbes.com/sites/dorie clark/2014/04/21/how-to-become-a-tedx-speaker/#1cc7a6171a3 [Online, accessed 16 September 2018]

Digital lens on the UKPSF. www.heacademy.ac.uk/system/files/downloads/ digital_lens_on_the_ukpsf.pdf [Online, accessed 16 September 2018].

Eraut, M. & Hirsh, W. (2007). *The Significance of Workplace Learning for Individuals, Groups and Organisations*. Oxford: SKOPE, Department of Economics, University of Oxford.

Jackson, N. (n.d.). *Ecology of Lifewide Learning & Personal/Professional Development*. www.normanjackson.co.uk/uploads/1/0/8/4/10842717/ecology_of_ lifewide_learning_final.pdf [Online, accessed 16 September 2018].

Practice and Evidence of the Scholarship of Teaching and Learning in Higher Education (PESTLHE). http://community.dur.ac.uk/pestlhe.learning/ index.php/pestlhe/index

QAA Scotland (2017). *Enhancement-led Institutional Review Handbook*.

Redecker, C., Leis, M., Leendertse, M., Punie, Y., Gijsbers, G., Kirschner, P., Stoyanov, S. & Hoogveld, B. (2011). *The Future of Learning. Preparing for Change*. Publications Office of the European Union. http://ftp.jrc.es/EUR doc/JRC66836.pdf [Online, accessed 16 September 2018]

TEDx. www.ted.com/tedx/events [Online, accessed 16 September 2018]

The Resilience Consortium. https://resilienceconsortium.bsc.harvard.edu [Online, accessed 16 September 2018].

The Higher Education Academy (2011). *UK Professional Standards Framework for Teaching and Supporting Learning in Higher Education* (UKPSF). York: The Higher Education Academy. www.heacademy.ac.uk/system/files/down loads/uk_professional_standards_framework.pdf [Online, accessed 16 September 2018].

VITAE (2018). Lenses on the VITAE Researcher Development Framework. www. vitae.ac.uk/researchers-professional-development/about-the-vitae- researcher-development-framework/lenses-on-the-vitae-researcher-develop ment-framework [Online, accessed 16 September 2018].

Chapter 12
Conclusion: A sense of direction

INTRODUCTION

Imagine arriving unexpectedly at a large intersection, with a whole series of different turnings that you could take. Some of the options would lead you straight into oncoming traffic, although you might not instantly be able to tell which ones these are; others would be safe to take, but lead you in the wrong direction, while one or two would actually get you to your destination. A clear sense of where you are headed, and a readiness to look at the road signs, would certainly help you in choosing the right route.

We have seen an array of ways to develop your teaching in this book. There are processes that rely on you taking the initiative, and those that are triggered by your professional responsibilities. Some processes involve colleagues, while others are more solitary. We have considered reflective approaches, and actions that you can carry out. The scale can range from significant ongoing responsibility for teaching to short exercises that you can carry out in five minutes. We have offered plenty of ideas for developing your teaching. But should you adopt this method from Chapter 5 or that strategy from Chapter 8? Should you embark on a project that will soak up all your 'spare' time, or review your existing practice instead? We need to ensure that we do more than randomly respond to circumstances.

In the first instance one can ask, what are the development processes that work for you, and in what circumstances? We are aware that our students need to understand how they learn if they are to manage their learning effectively and succeed in higher education; a similar principle holds for learning about our own teaching. Can you see any pattern emerging in the way you have responded to this book, and to the review points within it? Perhaps you expected us as authors to do all of the running, avoiding any activity on your own part. If you did try out a number

CONCLUSION: A SENSE OF DIRECTION

of the reviews, perhaps you can notice whether the ones you avoided had anything in common, or which ones benefited you the most; perhaps those involving interaction with colleagues. Megginson (1994) noted two patterns of learning that are particularly evident in the context of professional development: planned and emergent learning. He proposes that some people plan their learning quite deliberately, establishing at the outset the direction that their future learning will take and setting goals (see for instance development processes on pages 5–6 and 182–3). In contrast to such planned learning, others are ready take advantage of the opportunities to learn as they arise (evident on pages 126–8 and 175–9 amongst others). Megginson particularly encouraged learners to take on forms of learning to which they are not naturally inclined. You might thus try a specific exercise from within this book, perhaps one to which you are not naturally inclined, and then review what you learned from undertaking it.

We will, though, still find that several different development processes are likely to work in any given set of circumstances. Of course, we are all used to choosing from amongst a number of possible options – but what else guides us in these choices other than their immediate effectiveness? Are we left with an idiosyncratic approach, one that depends in large part on day-to-day whims, and that changes as our circumstances shift, perhaps with every new departmental policy or Vice-Chancellor? This concluding chapter looks at the nature of the overall choices you have to make about how to develop your teaching.

DEVELOPING YOUR TEACHING: AN ONGOING STORY

It is worth remembering that you are the one who makes the choices, and lives with the consequences. This means that there needs to be a match between your choices and what you genuinely value. We cannot simply look for a technical solution: a categorisation as a certain type of learner or a judgement as to the likely effectiveness of a given strategy. Palmer (2009) argued that understanding your own identity as a teacher is essential if you want to thrive, but this self-awareness is not something that is automatically ours. We need to explore what drives us if we are to understand which developments might turn out to be dead ends or lead us in the wrong direction altogether, resulting only in frustration.

Our aspirations for the future comprise a significant part of our identity as teachers and academics, helping us to determine where we are headed in developing our teaching. In many ways our aim is simply to teach well, and thus to help students learn effectively. In this book our primary focus has been on the process of developing your teaching. We could have tried to present an ideal vision of how to support student learning and then identified how to reach it, but instead we chose to focus on *how* to develop your teaching; on the process rather than on an end point. And yet our discussion has identified certain aspects of excellent teaching. It will be worth picking out some of the threads that have been evident within different chapters as to what genuinely good teaching might look like:

- **Excellent teaching maintains a focus on student learning.** It is the students who learn, and no teacher can force learning to occur.
- **Excellent teaching takes account of the discipline concerned.** It is essential for the methods that we employ to align themselves with the values that our disciplines hold dear. This has been particularly evident in the case studies.
- **Excellent teaching is a collaborative endeavour.** It stems from collaborations between colleagues and students, as we have seen in every single chapter; we work in a shared environment.
- **Excellent teaching challenges preconceived ideas.** A critical lens can be of great value in opening up new ways forward, ways that respond more effectively to the needs of learners or to society at large.

The characteristics of excellent teaching are, all the same, closely aligned with the process of developing your teaching: there is a synergy that is evident between them. Excellent teaching involves developing your teaching on an ongoing basis, given the pace of change in higher education and the need to maintain inspiration over the longer term. Snowden and McSherry (2017) argued that excellence is not a final destination, but rather a desired outcome that is constantly changing. Devlin and Samarawickrema (2010) similarly suggested that effective teaching has to evolve continually in order to respond to the changing world within which teaching and learning occurs. It is no coincidence that such factors as the student voice, the demands of the discipline and the contributions of colleagues feature in both the characteristics of excellent teaching and the processes by which teaching is best developed.

While we evidently need a clear set of aspirations or aims for the development of our teaching, our identity as someone who teaches will comprise far more than this. After all, my personal history will make it

CONCLUSION: A SENSE OF DIRECTION

more difficult to realise some aspirations than others. Your identity can be expressed in the form of an ongoing story, a narrative about your practice. The following questions provide prompts to help you articulate the story that underpins your teaching.

- What initially drew you to your discipline? What are the values held dear by this discipline? How can you reflect them more fully in your teaching? You might have been attracted to a discipline simply because you were good at it – but would this sustain your attempts to open it up to others as well?
- Why did you choose to teach? What are the major threads of your life that influence your teaching? Are there any important aspects of your life that have never had an opportunity to affect your teaching? Why not?
- To what extent is your identity rooted in your research? How does the relationship between your research and your teaching influence each other? What synergies can you exploit between these?
- What do you find compelling in your teaching? What is it in your teaching that your students react to with enthusiasm?
- What values underpin your teaching? Are you willing to take risks in order to help your students learn? Or would you rather play safe?

You might think of one or more critical incidents in your teaching that encapsulate your approach, or that help to illuminate each of these above questions, analysing the incidents in light of the advice given in Chapter 5. In Case study 12.1 Denise Batchelor begins to explore her own story by starting with a critical incident in her teaching.

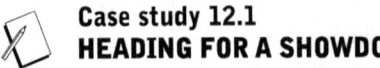

Case study 12.1
HEADING FOR A SHOWDOWN?

Denise Batchelor, Business, Computing and Information Management Faculty, London South Bank University

The discussion of Donne's sonnets was progressing well, with lively opinions being voiced by the seminar group. In the corner of the classroom stood a tall, dusty four-panelled black screen, abandoned after some past event. Within the

CONCLUSION: A SENSE OF DIRECTION

enclosure formed by the panels sat X, as he had done for the last five weeks, mostly silent, then suddenly, invisibly and aggressively stabbing angry and perceptive comments into the air.

The other students found the situation exasperating and amusing. I sensed their longing for me to confront X, insist that he conform, engineer a showdown. As a new and inexperienced lecturer my mind told me this is what a good teacher would do, what I should do. What would happen if the head of department heard that I was allowing a subversive student to lurk behind a screen, potentially sabotaging the smooth running of the class?

Something held me back. In week six X emerged and joined the class. Nothing was said publicly. Privately, X revealed that he had hated school, where he was labelled a failure and expelled for spectacular misbehaviour. He was building up to a similar dramatic scenario again. But something held him back.

Looking back at this nerve-racking incident many years later, I see now that any personal philosophy of teaching I have evolved since was present in embryo then, although as a novice I was acting purely and anxiously on instinct. Remembering this reminds me to try to tread carefully in mentoring staff and working with beginning teachers, to hold back from expressing my own ideas and interpretations too early, and to respect and trust colleagues' developing and different voices as they unpack and reflect on their experiences.

The value implicit in this episode that has become fundamentally important to me in subsequent years of teaching and, now, researching into the concept of student voice, is respect for students as individuals, seeking to:

- allow students space and freedom to be themselves rather than subscribing to a fixed idea of a student, an inflexible expectation of who and what students should be;
- accept students where they are;
- recognise that vulnerability in students manifests itself in unexpected ways;
- take risks;
- stay open to being surprised;
- have the courage to be myself in my teaching;
- listen to everything in a classroom, silences as well as words, in myself as well as my students.

A personal story can give meaning to your attempts to develop your teaching, as MacIntyre (2013: 250) notes: I can only answer the question

CONCLUSION: A SENSE OF DIRECTION

"What am I to do?" if I can answer the prior question "Of what story or stories do I find myself a part?"

An important part of our stories are the roles that both we and others play within them, as Denise evidently found. We can take a passive approach to a role that we take on, or engage more actively, as we saw in Chapter 9. All our stories involve other players as well, and their choices affect our choices as saw in Chapter 6. Just as the circumstances are given to us, so also the roles of those around us play an important part in shaping our story. You will thus also want to explore whether there are further networks, collaborative contexts or communities of practice in which you can participate more fully, or contexts in which you can take greater responsibility. When such social situations and roles align closely with your own aspirations and values, then coherence will certainly be added to the way in which you develop your teaching.

You may also find it helpful to move from creating a story to articulating your identity as a teacher in further ways. You might want to develop an action plan for the development of your teaching. Your goals, and the actions associated with them, need to be rooted quite clearly in your history and your present situation. Then, of course, you need to carry it out, reflecting on its usefulness and evaluating its effectiveness. Another option is to write a personal philosophy of teaching, and indeed of your teaching development. This would include attention to your conception of teaching, the methods you employ in teaching and in developing your teaching, and to the values and principles that underpin your practice, and its development.

Review point 12.1
A PERSONAL PHILOSOPHY

In order to create a personal philosophy of teaching, or personal philosophy of teaching development, you might reflect on the following.

- What method of teaching or developing your teaching do you rely on most frequently?
- Why don't you use another method?
- What do you think would happen if you changed that method?
- What does this tell you about your attitudes and approach towards student learning?

THE ROAD GOES EVER ON AND ON

A clearly articulated sense of identity as someone who develops their teaching, enables a further factor to come into play: the readiness to make choices that align with one's vision. A singleness of purpose can ensure that we are not blown around by every changing circumstance. As Palmer (2017) argued, it is integrity that enables us to remain true to our own stories as academics. Stories, action plans, personal philosophies and the roles that we play can all give unity to the way in which you develop your teaching. It is also true that a robust rationale for teaching can stem from these deeper representations of our identity.

A singleness of purpose is also developed through its public manifestations. How can we maintain a commitment to developing our teaching without colleagues (and students) finding out about it? We cannot do this on the quiet or, indeed, without trying to draw others in! Dissemination is not simply the icing on the cake, but an integral part of this work, as theories of the scholarship of teaching recognise. There are many ways to share our ideas and commitment with others, whether in corridor conversations, journal articles, blog postings, workshop discussions and so on.

We will certainly face many choices as to whether and how to develop our teaching: and indeed we have tried in this book to widen the choices that are open to you. Even with such choice, though, we still believe that it is possible to maintain a sense of the direction as you take forward your teaching. Give expression to a personal vision of how to develop your own teaching, and follow it along the road.

 REFERENCES

Devlin, M. & Samarawickrema, G. (2010). The criteria of effective teaching in a changing higher education context. *Higher Education Research & Development*, 29(2), 111–24.

MacIntyre, A. (2013). *After Virtue*. London: Bloomsbury.

Megginson, D. (1994). Planned and emergent learning: A framework and a method. *Executive Development*, 7(6), 29–32.

Palmer, P. J. (2009). *The Courage to Teach: Exploring the Inner Landscape of a Teacher's Life*. San Francisco, CA: John Wiley & Sons.

Snowden, M. & McSherry, R. (2017). Establishing excellence: Where do we go from here? In *The Pedagogy of the Social Sciences Curriculum* (pp. 107–18). Switzerland: Springer.

Glossary

Academic development – scholarly and institutional support to develop both educational practices and the capacities of educators in order to enhance student learning.

Action learning – a process that is conducted in a small group and based around real problems drawn from the activity of the participants. The process is designed to help those involved arrive at creative solutions to the challenges that are associated with their action.

Action research – a systematic process of self-reflective inquiry undertaken by those involved in carrying out a given set of actions in order to improve or enhance the quality or ethical standing of those actions. Action research often involves the direct participation of those affected by the action.

Advance HE – UK-based, sector-wide body with an increasingly international reach that aims to help shape the future of higher education, through providing insight, creating support, hosting networks and accrediting achievement.

AFHEA – Associate Fellow of the Higher Education Academy – accredited by Advance HE.

CPD – Continuing Professional Development.

Career-wide enhancement – an approach to personal and professional development that looks more widely at opportunities for enhancement than those embedded in a traditional, linear view of career progression.

Co-creation – working with our students in a variety of ways, from simple to highly involved partnerships, to develop teaching and learning approaches and/or resources.

Community of practice – a collection of people who share a profession or an area of human activity, and who together seek to advance their mutual practices.

GLOSSARY

Conception of teaching – a coherent set of meanings that are attached to the practice of teaching which mediate the response of the teacher. Such meanings may also be referred to as beliefs or abstract representations about teaching.

Constructive alignment – an approach to designing curricula that seeks to effect an alignment between intended learning outcomes, activities carried out by students and teachers, and assessment tasks. Alignment is said to be constructive given that it is the learner who constructs his or her own understanding.

Constructivism – as a philosophy of education, constructivism refers to the way in which those learning construct their own understanding through an interaction between their own experience and ideas. This process is often understood to occur on the basis of social interaction with others.

Critical community – a stable group in which attention is focused on the group as a whole, taking in debate, critique and learning about the practices pursued within the group.

Critical pedagogy – teaching and learning that questions in an egalitarian fashion the status quo in operation within the social setting inhabited by the students and teachers, taking particular account of the aspirations and needs of the students.

Deep approach to learning – tasks are carried out by students in ways that both prioritise the development of understanding and manifest a genuine interest in the subject of study.

Deliberate practice – an approach to continuing professional development, linked to developing expertise, which places an emphasis on time, feedback, focus and motivation from the individual.

Distributed leadership – the process by which senior leaders devolve some aspects of leadership to others or the process by which new leaders emerge through the exercise of bottom-up influence rather than through the exercise of a formal authority.

EDUCAUSE – non-profit association which aims to advance the cause of higher education through the use of information technology. Produces the annual NMC Horizon Reports which provide a community view from a panel of experts on profiled topics that are predicted to have a significant impact on higher education practice over the forthcoming five years in relation to information technology.

Employability – an ongoing reflective approach to developing personal attributes and capacities that are transferable and adaptive, enabling positive engagement in the job market.

GLOSSARY

Enquiry-based learning – an umbrella term to describe approaches to learning that are driven by a process of enquiry. This may include engagement with an open-ended scenario in which students (often in small groups) direct the lines of enquiry and the methods employed, and report on their findings.

Enterprise – an approach that is built into a curriculum in order to support students in developing a proactive approach to their studies and to their employability skills.

Excellence in teaching & learning – much sought after in higher education. Many claims are made to measure excellence in teaching & learning and to recognise and reward its existence but it remains a highly contested concept. Best sought and realised through practical expression in student learning.

Expansive learning – learning that occurs in unexpected places, and at times that cannot easily be predicted in advance or directly controlled by teachers.

Experiential learning – a process of learning through reflection on experience, entailing experience that is itself actively shaped and transformed.

Feedforward – comments, suggestions and advice provided to students on how they might further develop and enhance their work; as opposed to feedback on the current piece of work.

FHEA – Fellow of the Higher Education Academy – accredited by Advance HE.

Flipped learning/classroom – an approach to teaching and learning by which students engage with curriculum content prior to a class, with contact time with teachers used for discussion and interaction around that content.

High-impact practices – educational practices that have been linked to high levels of student engagement and retention, including those practices that emphasise writing processes, collaborative assignments and projects, service learning and work placements.

Higher Education Academy (HEA) – part of three nested brands within Advance HE, alongside the Leadership Foundation and the Equality Challenge Unit. Continues to provide its name to the Fellowship framework.

ISB – International Student Barometer, a student survey seeking feedback on the international student experience. It is used as a global benchmarking tool.

Learning outcome – an (intended) learning outcome is a concise description of what a student should have learnt at the end of a learning process. It typically includes an active verb (often with an associated adverb), an object of the verb and a phrase that indicates the context or provides a condition.

GLOSSARY

Learning style – contested theoretical concept that identifies a preferential way in which a student develops understanding or expertise. Teachers may be expected to adapt their teaching methods to take into account the range of learning styles characterised by a given model. Value arguably remains in the concept with regard to its usefulness in highlighting to students that there is no one 'right way' to learn and in encouraging them to explore and begin to understand the ways in which they learn most effectively.

NMC Horizon Reports – New Media Consortium, now part of EDUCAUSE, produces a range of reports which provide a view of potential disruptive technologies in relation to learning and teaching across all educational sectors.

NSS – National Student Survey of final year students in the UK. Has come under some criticism for being a student satisfaction survey but is influential in relation to league tables and rankings.

NSSE – National Survey of Student Engagement is a survey tool used in the USA and Canada to measure students' participation in relation to learning and engagement.

Padlet – a commercial tool which provides an online virtual bulletin board which can be used for planning, collaboration, feedback, etc.

Participative inquiry – a process of inquiry in which students are equal participants in their own educational experience.

Philosophy of teaching – a self-reflective statement of one's beliefs or core ideas about teaching and learning, along with a justification of the appropriateness of those beliefs, which adapts and develops throughout a teaching career

PFHEA – Principal Fellow of the Higher Education Academy – accredited by Advance HE.

Problem-based learning – an approach to learning in which the handling of a set of problems defines and drives the entire learning experience for small groups of students. Students define for themselves the emerging issues, seek out further knowledge and present on their resulting understanding. The curriculum is structured by the problems rather than by systematic presentation of subject content.

Reflective practice – a critical learning 'conversation' with ourselves or others that can take a variety of forms, with the object of enhancing our practice. Often facilitated by reflective models.

Reflexivity – a meta-cognitive approach undertaken within professional practice to support interrogation and resolution of challenges within an environment of super-complexity.

GLOSSARY

Scholarship of teaching and learning (SoTL) – systematic and informed inquiry into one's teaching or into the learning of one's students carried out in order to enhance that learning. The results of such inquiry are then shared with others.

Self-efficacy – the belief that you can achieve what you set out to do. An individual's belief in his or her innate ability to achieve goals. It entails a personal judgement of how well one can execute courses of action required to deal with prospective situations.

SFHEA – Senior Fellow of the Higher Education Academy – accredited by Advance HE.

Signature pedagogy – a form of teaching that characteristically applies to a given discipline or profession.

Social practice theory – a theory that highlights how knowing and doing are intertwined with each other, along with the relationships, interactions, infrastructures and material conditions that accompany the practice.

Student engagement – the exercise of intentional action by a student within a given environment for learning. Where student engagement is considered from the viewpoint of an institution, attention may be specifically devoted to considering the way in which the investment of both students and the institution leads to high quality learning outcomes or student experiences.

Surface approach to learning – tasks undertaken by a student are focused on reproducing information that has been provided to them.

Threshold concept – an idea that is fundamental to understanding or progress in a given area of study.

Virtual learning environment – a centrally managed Web-based platform that hosts resources, activities and assessments within the structure of a course, in order to enhance students' experience of education.

WonkHE – UK-based, predominantly online forum for the discussion of all matters relating to higher education. Non-partisan platform with a mission to improve policy making in higher education.

Index

action learning 92–3, 110, 128, 173
action planning 5–6, 81, 182–3, 190
active learning 12–13, 16, 17, 32–3, 49, 52–3, 57, 69–70, 82, 103, 109
Advance HE 20, 45, 111, 113, 160, 193; *see also* Higher Education Academy
approaches to learning *see* learning, approaches to
arts 28, 34, 41–2, 50–2, 125
assessment 21, 24–5, 33, 34, 40, 58, 88, 111, 125
assumptions 22, 73, 75, 82, 83
authentic learning 40, 49, 57, 61–4

careers in teaching xvi, 90, 108, 166–7, 176, 193
Carnegie Foundation for the Advancement of Teaching 113
co-construction of education 46–57, 193
collaboration 18, 34, 38, 58, 85, 87–8, 126, 139
communities: critical 38, 41, 194; of practice 34–8, 120, 193
conceptions of teaching *see* teaching, conceptions of
consumerism 4, 49
constructive alignment 19, 21, 25, 45, 124, 194
constructivisim 22, 194

critical incidents 73, 188–9
critical pedagogy 22–3, 37–8, 78, 194
critical thinking 12, 37
culture in teaching 12–13, 37, 74, 117
curriculum 6, 22, 40, 46, 50–6, 60, 64, 87–9, 134

deep approach to learning *see* learning, approaches to
deliberate practice 155–8, 166
department 11, 16, 23, 34–8, 56, 85, 89, 104; high-performing 131, 138
design 30, 51–2, 61–2
dialogue 22, 28, 34–8, 89, 98, 149
disciplines 7, 21, 22–3, 63, 86, 89, 92, 122, 188; as a basis for engagement 27–33; *see also* under specific discipline
disciplinary practices 29–31, 34, 35
dissemination 160, 175, 178, 179, 180, 191
drivers for change 6, 39–40, 46–7, 52, 87, 100–14, 139
double-loop learning 71, 76

e-portfolios 2, 169, 183
educational research 7, 23, 116–8, 121–8, 137; groups 127; *see also* practitioner research

199

INDEX

educational theory 20, 21, 22–3, 27, 29, 67, 71, 78, 94, 123–4; *see also* theory
emergent learning 5, 52, 134, 186
emotions 42, 110, 149
employability 6, 12, 33, 38, 39–40, 47–8, 56, 62, 91–2, 97, 194; *see also* work-based learning
English studies 28, 122, 188–9
engagement *see* student engagement
enquiry-based learning 19, 28, 34, 36–7, 194
environmental sciences 36–7; *see also* fieldwork
evaluation 20, 38, 66–7, 105, 107, 110, 118–21
excellence *see* teaching excellence
expansive learning 41–2, 194
experiential learning 14, 32, 70–1, 83

feedback *see* student feedback
fieldwork 18–19, 30, 147; *see also* environmental studies
flipped learning 16, 32, 104, 194

group work 12, 21, 33, 50, 103–4, 109; *see also* large groups
graduate teaching assistants 57–8, 96, 140–2, 162–3

healthcare 97–8, 143, 158–9
Higher Education Academy 16, 39, 59, 60, 64, 142, 146, 147, 195; *see also* Advance HE
Higher Education Research and Development Society of Australasia 113
high-impact practices 101, 116, 194

identity 1, 77, 127, 186–7
immersive learning 42, 87
inclusivity 8, 34, 36–8, 64, 78, 159–60, 176–7
innovation 23, 74–5, 85–6, 117, 118–9, 121, 126

institutional perspectives 23, 35–6, 38, 86, 89, 112, 127, 136, 166
interdisciplinary working 86, 88
internationalisation 8, 35, 37, 60, 76, 146

journals *see* learning journals

Kolb's model of learning 70–2

laboratory teaching 29–30, 86
language learning 36, 136–7
large groups 16, 33, 75–6, 103, 134
leadership 131–2, 136–44; agenda 135–9; communication in 139–40; distributed 140, 194
learning: approaches to 124, 194, 197; environments 13, 18–19, 30, 37, 50, 52, 82, 85, 97, 105, 110; journals 67, 73, 77, 78, 183; materials 72, 89, 94, 95–6, 126, 137–8; outcomes 10–11, 13, 19, 20, 22, 25, 28, 55, 195; styles 124, 195; *see also* under specific type of learning
lectures 12, 17, 18, 19, 20, 25, 29–30, 39, 49, 79–80, 103, 109
legal studies 20
lifelong learning 47, 167
lifewide learning 83, 167, 175–8

management studies 15, 32, 35, 134
materiality 29, 37, 86
materials *see* learning materials
mathematics 30, 123
medicine 30, 97–8
mentoring 17, 52–3, 79, 91–2, 141, 159, 172–3

National Student Survey *see* surveys
networking 90–1, 154, 157, 180–1
novice, teaching as a 27, 148–9, 183

observation of teaching *see* peer observation
occupational therapy 82–3

200

INDEX

online education 2, 15–16, 24, 46, 72, 74, 87–8, 168
outdoor education 36–7, 147

part-time teachers 90
partnerships 4, 40, 47; *see also* student partnerships
peer learning 39–40, 59, 82
peer observation 17–18, 73, 79–81, 157
philosophy of teaching 3, 6, 108, 110, 189–90, 196
planned learning 186
PowerPoint 13, 32, 51, 74, 109, 119–20
practitioner research 117, 179; see *also* educational research
professional development 4–5, 52, 69, 79, 97–8, 101, 125, 156–7, 167, 168, 171; frameworks for 173–5, 181–3; *see also* programmes in learning and teaching
programmes in learning and teaching 12–13, 14, 17, 21, 22–3, 24–5, 58–9, 66, 79–80, 122, 123–4, 167–8
problem-based learning 40, 62, 143, 196
psychology 39–40, 141
publication 6, 118, 123, 127, 143, 179

qualifications *see* programmes in learning and teaching
quality assurance 28, 87, 132, 161

reflection *see* reflective practice
refletive practice 5, 6, 14, 21, 23, 59, 81; criticality in relation to 81–2, 196; in relation to action 68–70, 107–8; terminology of 66–7
reflexivity 110, 162, 196
relationships in teaching and learning 4, 89–93, 140, 172–3

research and teaching 86–7, 134
researching teaching and learning *see* educational research
resources *see* learning materials
roles 91–2, 131–5, 190

scholarship of teaching and learning 7, 8, 117–8, 179, 197
sciences 29, 34, 36, 39, 55–6, 121, 162–3
self-efficacy 95, 98, 116, 159, 197
service learning 101, 116
signature pedagogies 3, 29, 30, 41–2, 197
skills *see* student skills
social media 52–3, 58, 90
social practice theory 29, 197
social sciences 34, 39, 77, 121
spatiality 37, 41, 47, 61–2, 86, 103–4
staff development *see* professional development
student-centred learning and teaching 3, 19, 21, 35–6, 37, 49–50, 62, 69, 187, 189
student: engagement 27–33, 37–8, 39, 45–7, 52, 55–6, 62, 116, 141, 197; feedback 33, 50–1, 70, 71–2, 74, 93; partnerships 8, 15–16, 41, 45–6, 104–5, 120; skills 12, 13, 19, 28, 33, 39–40, 47–8, 59, 62, 148–9, 162; support 56, 141; voice 3, 60, 105; see also co-construction of education
subject-specific approaches to teaching *see* disciplines
surface approach to learning *see* learning, approaches to
surveys 45, 101, 104, 146, 196

teaching: awards 153–4, 160, 177; conceptions of 31–2, 34, 49, 149, 194; fellowships 160–1; from the microcosm 30; philosophy *see* philosophy of teaching;

INDEX

qualifications *see* programmes in learning and teaching
teaching excellence 1, 7, 23, 27, 30, 35, 128, 131, 136, 187, 194; definitions of 146–7, 153; measurement of 147, 152; models of 148–9, 153
Teaching Excellence Framework 146–7
team teaching 3, 8, 18, 87–8, 89, 96–7, 137–8
technology 41–2, 71–2, 88, 112–12, 116–17, 118–19; *see also* under specific technology
temporality 37, 41, 103, 118

theory: espoused 32, 75–6; *see also* educational theory
threshold concepts 34
transformative learning 46

values 63–4, 81, 108, 149, 167, 174–5, 187–8, 190
veterinary education 58–9
videos 2, 16, 33, 56, 74, 81, 109
Virtual Learning Environment (VLE) 72, 112, 138, 169, 197

work-based learning 6, 47, 97–8, 101, 116; *see also* employability
workshops 32, 59, 69, 89, 178

For Product Safety Concerns and Information please contact our EU representative GPSR@taylorandfrancis.com
Taylor & Francis Verlag GmbH, Kaufingerstraße 24, 80331 München, Germany

www.ingramcontent.com/pod-product-compliance
Lightning Source LLC
Chambersburg PA
CBHW050633300426
44112CB00012B/1781